NECRONS

By Matthew Ward

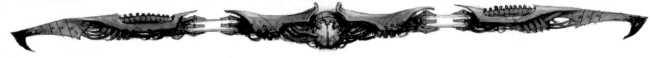

CONTENTS

Art: John Blanche, Alex Boyd, Kevin Chin, Paul Dainton, Dave Gallagher, Neil Hodgson, Nuala Kinrade, John Michelbach, Adrian Smith. **Book Design:** Christian Byrne, Carl Dafforn, Glenn More, Emma Parrington, Mark Raynor. **'Eavy Metal:** Neil Green, David Heathfield, Mark Holmes, Kornel Kozak, Darren Latham, Joe Tomaszewski, Anja Wettergren. **Games Development:** Robin Cruddace, Matthew Hobday, Jervis Johnson, Phil Kelly, Mark Latham, Adam Troke, Jeremy Vetock, Sarah Wallen, Matthew Ward. **Additional Playtesting:** Tris Buckroyd, Paul Hickey, Matt Hilton, Martin Morrin, Gary Shaw. **Miniatures Design:** Mike Anderson, Giorgio Bassani, Trish Carden, Juan Diaz, Martin Footitt, **Hobby Team:** Dave Andrews, Mark Jones, Chad Mierzwa, Chris Peach, Duncan Rhodes. Mike Fores, Jes Goodwin, Colin Grayson, Mark Harrison, Alex Hedström, Matt Holland, Neil Langdown, Aly Morrison, Brian Nelson, Oliver Norman, Seb Perbet, Alan Perry, Michael Perry, Dale Stringer, Dave Thomas, Tom Walton. **Production & Reprographics:** Simon Burton, Chris Eggar, Marc Elliott, Zaff Haydn-Davies, Kris Jaggers, Melissa Roberts, Rachel Ryan, James Shardlow, Markus Trenkner. **Previous Editions:** Andy Chambers, Pete Haines, Andy Hoare, Phil Kelly, Graham McNeill. **Special Thanks to:** Andrew Kenrick, Alan Merrett, Rick Priestley.

UK
Games Workshop Ltd.,
Willow Rd, Lenton,
Nottingham,
NG7 2WS

NORTHERN EUROPE
Games Workshop Ltd.,
Willow Rd, Lenton,
Nottingham,
NG7 2WS

NORTH AMERICA
Games Workshop Inc,
6211 East Holmes Road,
Memphis,
Tennessee 38141

AUSTRALIA
Games Workshop,
23 Liverpool Street,
Ingleburn,
NSW 2565

INTRODUCTION

The Necrons are the amongst the most ancient of all the galaxy's races. Awoken from hibernation, and driven by a command they cannot deny, they now march forth to reconquer their lost dynasties and destroy any race foolish enough to block their path.

THE WARHAMMER 40,000 GAME

The *Warhammer 40,000* rulebook contains the rules you need to fight battles with your Citadel miniatures set in the war-torn universe of the 41st Millennium. Every army has its own codex that works alongside these rules, allowing you to turn your collection of miniatures into an organised army for your games of Warhammer 40,000. This codex details everything you need to know about the ancient Necrons.

WHY COLLECT A NECRON ARMY?

The Necrons were once the rulers of the galaxy. For long aeons they slumbered in their stasis-crypts, waiting for the galaxy to recover from the terrible war that almost tore it asunder. Now the Necrons are waking from their dormancy. They seek to destroy the lesser life forms that infest their old domains, and re-establish their rightful rule.

The Necrons are masters of ranged combat and win their battles through overwhelming firepower – indeed, their ranged weaponry can be ranked amongst the most powerful in the Warhammer 40,000 game. Whether you're resolutely defending a crucial location or implacably advancing on a vital stronghold, you'll drive the enemy before you with the torrents of gauss- and tesla-fire of Necron Warriors, Deathmarks and Immortals. Should these not prove sufficient to the task at hand, stranger and more destructive weaponry is available to you in the form of the Monolith's particle whip, the Doomsday Ark's unbelievably destructive cannon, or the reality-warping techno-sorcery of the Crypteks.

Only in the bitter melee of close combat are your Necrons truly vulnerable, but to get into assault range your foe must first survive their precision volleys. Even then, Necrons are difficult to destroy – and they don't always stay down. In the later turns of the game, when your opponent's army has been worn away by the grind of battle (and your expert generalship) your Necrons will still stand strong, ready to defeat any troops he has left to throw at you.

HOW THIS CODEX WORKS

Codex: Necrons contains the following sections:

The Necrons: This section introduces the Necrons, their place in the Warhammer 40,000 universe and their quest to reclaim the galaxy. Here you will learn of their history and royal dynasties, their strongholds and great campaigns.

The Army of Aeons Past: Here you will find a full examination of every character, squad and vehicle in the Necron army. Firstly, you will find a full description of the unit detailing its role within the Necron legions as well as its specialised combat abilities. Secondly, you will discover complete rules for the unit, including any unique wargear or special abilities it can bring to bear.

Awakening the Tomb: This section contains colour photographs of the extensive range of Citadel miniatures available for your Necron army, gloriously painted by Games Workshop's 'Eavy Metal team.

Wargear: In this section, you'll find full details and rules for the incredible battlefield technologies employed by the Necrons, from gauss flayers and voidblades to disruption fields and tesseract labyrinths.

Necrons Army List: The army list takes all the units presented in the Army of Aeons Past section and arranges them so you can choose an army for your own games. Each unit type also has an associated points value to help you pit your forces against an opponent's in a fair match.

FIND OUT MORE

Codex: Necrons contains everything you need to play a game with your army, but there are always more tactics to try, scenarios to fight and painting ideas to explore. The monthly White Dwarf magazine contains articles about all aspects of the Warhammer 40,000 game and hobby, and you can also find articles specific to the Necrons on our website:

www.games-workshop.com

THE NECRONS

Across the galaxy, an ancient and terrible race is stirring. Entombed in stasis-crypts, they have slumbered through the aeons, waiting for the galaxy to heal from the wounds of a long and bloody war. Now, after sixty million years of dormancy, a great purpose begins. On desolate worlds thought long-bereft of life, ancient machineries wake into grim function, commencing the slow processes of revivification that will see those entombed within freed to stride across the stars once again. The implacable Necron legions are rising. Let the galaxy beware.

All Necrons, from the lowliest of warriors to the most regal of lords, are driven by one ultimate goal, to restore their ancient dynasties to glory – to bring the galaxy under their rule once more. Such was the edict long ago encoded into the Necrons' minds, and it is a command so fundamental to their being that it cannot be denied. Yet it is no small task, for the Necrons are awakening from their Tomb Worlds to find the galaxy much changed. Many Tomb Worlds are no more, destroyed by cosmic disaster or alien invasion. Others are damaged, their entombed legions afflicted by slow madness or worn to dust by entropy's irresistible onset. Degenerate alien races squat amongst the ruins of those Necron Tomb Worlds that remain, little aware of the greatness they defile with their upstart presence. Yet there is no salvation to be found in such ignorance. The dead have come to reclaim their lands, and the living shall be swept aside.

Yet if billions of Necrons have been destroyed by the passage of eternity, countless billions more remain to see their dominion reborn. They are not creatures of flesh and blood, these Necrons, but android warriors whose immortal forms are forged from living metal. As such, they are almost impervious to destruction, and their bodies are swift to heal even the gravest wounds. Given time, severed limbs reattach, armour plating reknits and shattered mechanical organs are rebuilt. The only way, then, to assure a Necron's destruction is to overwhelm its ability to self-repair, to inflict such massive damage that its systems cannot keep pace. Even then, should irreparable damage occur, the Necron will often simply 'phase out' – automated teleport beams returning it to the safety of the stasis-crypts, where it remains in storage until such time as repairs can be carried out.

The sciences by which such feats are achieved remain a mystery to outsiders, for the Necrons do not share their secrets with lesser races and have set contingencies to prevent their supreme technologies from falling into the wrong hands. Should a fallen warrior fail to phase out, it self-destructs and is consumed by a blaze of emerald light. Outwardly, this appears little different to the glow of teleportation, leaving the foe to wonder whether the Necron has finally been destroyed or has merely retreated to its tomb. Victory over the Necrons is therefore a tenuous thing, and a hard-won battle grants little surety of ultimate victory. For the Necrons, defeats are minor inconveniences – the preludes to future triumphs, nothing more. Immortality has brought patience; the perils that the Necrons survived in ancient times carry the lesson that their race can overcome any opposition, if they have but the will to try. And if the Necrons possess only a single trait, it is a will as unbending as adamantium.

Only one hope can now preserve the other races from the Necrons' implacable advance, from the endless legions of silent and deathless warriors rising from long-forgotten tombs. If the Necrons can be prevented from waking to their full glory, if the scattered Tomb Worlds can be prevented from unifying, then there is a chance of survival. If not, then the great powers of the galaxy will surely fall, and the Necrons shall rule supreme for eternity.

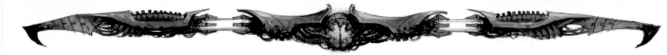

IN THE BEGINNING

The race that would become the Necrons began their existence under a fearsome, scourging star, billions of years before Mankind evolved on Terra. Assailed at every moment by solar winds and radiation storms, the flesh and blood Necrontyr became a morbid people whose precarious life spans were riven by constant loss. Their dynasties were founded on the anticipation of demise, and the living were thought of as no more than temporary residents hurrying through the sepulchres and tombs of their ancestors.

Unable to find peace on their own planet, the Necrontyr blindly groped out towards other worlds. Using stasis-crypts aboard slow burning torch-ships, they began to colonise other planets. Little by little, the Necrontyr dynasties spread ever further, until much of the galaxy answered to their rule.

THE FIRST WARS OF SECESSION

As time wore on, further strife came to the Necrontyr. As their territory grew ever wider and more diverse, the unity that had made them strong was eroded, and bitter wars were raged as entire realms fought to win independence. Ultimately, the Triarch – the ruling council of the Necrontyr – realised that the only hope of unity lay in conflict with an external enemy, but there were few who could prove a credible threat. Only the Old Ones, first of all the galaxy's sentient life, were a prospective foe great enough to bind the Necrontyr to a common cause. Such a war was simplicity itself to justify, for the Necrontyr had ever rankled at the Old Ones' refusal to share the secrets of eternal life. So did the Triarch declare war upon the Old Ones. At the same time, they offered amnesty to any secessionist dynasties who willingly returned to the fold. Thus lured by the spoils of victory and the promise of immortality, the separatist realms abandoned rebellion and the War in Heaven began.

THE WAR IN HEAVEN

The terrible campaigns that followed could fill a library in their own right, but the underlying truth was a simple one: the Necrontyr could never win. Their superior numbers and technologies were constantly outmanoeuvred by the Old Ones' mastery of the webway portals. In but a span of centuries, the Necrontyr were pushed back until they were little more than an irritation, a quiescent peril clinging to isolated and forgotten worlds. In the face of defeat, the unity of the Necrontyr began to fracture once more. No longer did the prospect of a common enemy have any hold over the disparate dynasties. Scores of generations had now lived and died in the service of an unwinnable war, and many Necrontyr dynasties would have gladly sued for peace had the ruling Triarch permitted it.

Thus began the second iteration of the Wars of Secession, more widespread and ruinous than any that had come before. So fractured had the Necrontyr dynasties become by then that, had the Old Ones been so inclined, they could have wiped them out with ease. Faced with the total collapse of their rule, the Triarch searched desperately for a means of restoring order. In this, their prayers were answered, though the price would be incalculably high.

THE COMING OF THE C'TAN

It was during the reign of Szarekh that the godlike energy beings known as the C'tan first blighted the Necrontyr. It is impossible to say for certain how the Necrontyr first came to encounter the C'tan, though many misleading, contradictory and one-sided accounts of these events exist. The dusty archives of Solemnace claim it was but an accident, a chance discovery made by a stellar probe during the investigation of a dying star. The Book of Mournful Night, held under close guard in the Black Library's innermost sanctum, tells rather that the raw hatred that the Necrontyr held for the Old Ones sang out across space, acting as a beacon the C'tan could not ignore. Howsoever contact occurred, the shadow of the C'tan fell over the oldest dynasties first. Some Necrontyr actively sought the C'tan's favour and oversaw the forging of living metal bodies to contain the star-gods' nebulous essence. Thus clad, the C'tan took the shapes of the Necrontyr's half-forgotten gods, hiding their own desires beneath cloaks of obsequious subservience.

So it was that one of the C'tan came before the Silent King, acting as forerunner to the coming of his brothers. Amongst its own kind, this C'tan was known as the Deceiver, for it was wilfully treacherous. Yet the Silent King knew not the C'tan's true nature, and instead granted the creature an audience. The Deceiver spoke of a war, fought long before the birth of the Necrontyr, between the C'tan and the Old Ones. It was a war, he said, that the C'tan had lost. In the aftermath, and fearing the vengeance of the Old Ones, he and his brothers had hidden themselves away, hoping one day to find allies with whom they could finally bring the Old Ones to account. In return for aid, the Deceiver assured, he and his brothers would deliver everything that the Necrontyr craved. Unity could be theirs once again, and the immortality that they had sought for so long would finally be within their grasp. No price would there be for these great gifts, the Deceiver insisted, for they were but boons to be bestowed upon valued allies.

Thus did the Deceiver speak, and who can say how much of his tale was truth? It is doubtful whether even the Deceiver knew, for trickery had become so much a part of his existence that even he could no longer divine its root. Yet his words held sway over Szarekh who, like his ancestors before him, despaired of the divisions that were tearing his people apart. For long months he debated the matter with the Triarch and the nobles of his Royal Court. Through it

THE TRIARCH AND THE SILENT KING

From the earliest days, the rulers of individual Necrontyr dynasties were themselves governed by the Triarch, a council of three Phaerons. The head of the Triarch was known as the Silent King, for he addressed his subjects only through the other two Phaerons who ruled alongside him. Nominally a hereditary position, the uncertain life spans of the Necrontyr ensured that the title of Silent King nonetheless passed from one royal dynasty to another many times. The final days of the Necrontyr occur in the reign of Szarekh, last of the Silent Kings.

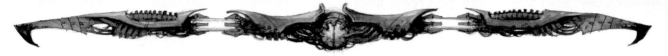

all, the only dissenting voice was that of Orikan, the court astrologer, who foretold that the alliance would bring about a renaissance of glory, but destroy forever the soul of the Necrontyr people. Yet desire and ambition swiftly overrode caution, and Orikan's prophecy was dismissed. A year after the Deceiver had presented his proposition, the Triarch agreed to the alliance, and so forever doomed their race.

BIOTRANSFERENCE

With the pact between Necrontyr and C'tan sealed, the star gods revealed the form that immortality would take, and the great biotransference began. Colossal bio-furnaces roared day and night, consuming weak-bodied flesh and replacing it with enduring forms of living metal. As the cyclopean machines clamoured, the C'tan swarmed about the biotransference sites, drinking in the torrent of cast-off life energy and growing ever stronger.

As Szarekh watched the C'tan feast on the life essence of his people, he realised the terrible depth of his mistake. In many ways, he felt better than he had in decades, the countless aches and uncertainties of organic life now behind him. His new machine body was far mightier than the frail form he had tolerated for so long, and his thoughts were swifter and clearer than they had ever been. Yet there was an emptiness gnawing at his mind, an inexpressible hollowness of spirit that defied rational explanation. In that moment, he knew with cold certainty that the price of physical immortality had been the loss of his soul. With great sorrow the Silent King beheld the fate he had brought upon his people: the Necrontyr were now but a memory, and the soulless Necrons reborn in their place.

Yet if the price had been steep, biotransference had fulfilled all of the promises that the C'tan had made. Even the lowliest of Necrontyr was blessed with immortality – age and radiation could little erode their new bodies, and only the most terrible of injuries could destroy them utterly. Likewise, the Necrons enjoyed a unity that the Necrontyr had never known, though it was achieved through tyranny rather than consent. The biotransference process had embedded command protocols in every mind, granting Szarekh the unswerving loyalty of his subjects. At first, the Silent King embraced this unanimity, for it was a welcome reprieve from the chaos of recent years. However, as time wore on he grew weary of his burden but dared not sever the command protocols, lest his subjects turn on him seeking vengeance for the terrible curse he had visited upon them.

THE OLD ONES DEFEATED

With the C'tan and the Necrons fighting as one, the Old Ones were now doomed to defeat. Glutted on the life force of the Necrontyr, the empowered C'tan were nigh unstoppable and unleashed forces beyond comprehension. Planets were razed, suns extinguished and whole systems devoured by black holes called into being by the reality warping powers of the star gods. Necron legions finally broached the webway and assailed the Old Ones in every

> 'When the Silent King saw what had been done, he knew at last the true nature of the C'tan, and of the doom they had wrought in his name.'
>
> - excerpt from the Book of Mournful Night

corner of the galaxy. They brought under siege the fortresses of the Old Ones' allies, harvesting the life force of the defenders to feed their masters. Ultimately, beset by the implacable onset of the C'tan and the calamitous Warp-spawned perils they had themselves mistakenly unleashed, the Old Ones were defeated, scattered and finally destroyed.

THE SILENT KING'S BETRAYAL

Throughout the final stages of the War in Heaven, Szarekh bided his time, waiting for the moment in which the C'tan would be vulnerable. Though the entire Necron race was his to command, he could not hope to oppose the C'tan at the height of their power, and even if he did and met with success, the Necrons would then have to finish the War in Heaven alone. No, the Old Ones had to be defeated before the C'tan could be brought to account for the horror they had wrought. And so, when the C'tan finally won their great war, their triumph was short lived. With one hated enemy finally defeated, and the other spent from hard-fought victory, the Silent King at last led the Necrons in revolt.

In their arrogance, the C'tan did not realize their danger until it was too late. The Necrons focussed the unimaginable energies of the living universe into weapons too mighty for even the C'tan to endure. Alas, the C'tan were immortal star-spawn, part of the fundamental fabric of actuality and therefore nigh impossible to destroy. So was each C'tan instead sundered into thousands of fragments. Yet this was sufficient to the Silent King's goals. Indeed, he had known the C'tan's ultimate destruction to be impossible and had drawn his plans accordingly: each C'tan Shard was bound within a tesseract labyrinth, as trammelled and secure as a genie in a bottle. Though the cost of victory was high – millions had been destroyed as a consequence of rebellion, including all of the Triarch save the Silent King himself – the Necrons were once more in command of their own destiny.

THE GREAT SLEEP

Yet even with the defeat of the Old Ones and the C'tan alike, the Silent King saw that the time of the Necrons was over – for the moment, at least. The mantle of galactic dominion would soon pass to the Eldar, a race who had fought alongside the Old Ones throughout the War in Heaven and had thus come to hate the Necrons and all their works. The Eldar had survived where the Old Ones had not and the Necrons, weakened during the overthrow of the C'tan, could not stand against them. Yet the Silent King knew that the time of the Eldar would pass, as did the time of all flesh.

So it was that the Silent King ordered the remaining Necron cities to be transformed into great tomb complexes threaded with stasis-crypts. Let the Eldar shape the galaxy for a time – they were but ephemeral, whilst the Necrons were eternal. The Silent King's final command to his people was that they must sleep for sixty million years but awake ready to rebuild all that they had lost, to restore the dynasties to their former glory. Thus was the Silent King's last order, and as the last Tomb World sealed its vaults, he destroyed the command protocols by which he had controlled his people, for he had failed them utterly. Without a backward glance, Szarekh, last of the Silent Kings, took ship into the blackness of intergalactic space, there to find whatever measure of solace or penance he could.

Meanwhile, aeons passed, and the Necrons slept on...

THE GREAT AWAKENING

None can say for sure how many Tomb Worlds entered the Great Sleep, but it is certain that a great many did not survive into the 41st Millennium. Technologically advanced though the Necrons were, to attempt a stasis-sleep of such scale was a great risk, even for them.

For sixty million years the Necrons slept, voicelessly waiting for their chance to complete the Silent King's final order: to restore the Necron dynasties to their former glory. As the centuries passed, ever more Tomb Worlds fell prey to malfunction or ill-fortune. For many, the results were minor, such as a disruption to the operation of the Tomb World's chronostat or revivification chambers, causing the inhabitants to awaken later than intended – but some Tomb Worlds suffered more calamitous events.

Cascade failures of stasis-crypts destroyed millions, if not billions, of dormant Necrons. Some Tomb Worlds were destroyed by the retribution of marauding Eldar, their defence systems overmatched by these ancient enemies. Other Tomb Worlds fell victim to the uncaring evolution of the galaxy itself. Tectonically unstable planets crushed Necron strongholds slumbering at their hearts; stars went supernova, consuming orbiting Tomb Worlds in their death throes. And everywhere, inquisitive life forms scrabbled and fought over the bones of the Necron territories, causing more damage in their unthinking search for knowledge than the vengeful Eldar ever could.

RISING FROM OBLIVION

The awakening has been far from precise, and the Necrons have not arisen as one but in fitful starts over scattered millennia, like some gestalt sleeper rising from a troubled dream. Errors in circuitry and protocols ensured that a revivification destined to take place in the early years of M41 actually began far earlier in a few cases, or has yet to occur at all in others. The very first Tomb Worlds revived to see the Great Crusade sweep across the galaxy. A handful stirred in time to see Nova Terra challenge the might of the Golden Throne, or arose at the hour in which the Apostles of the Blind King waged their terrible wars. Some have never awoken. Even now, at the close of the 41st Millennium, billions of Necrons still slumber in their tombs, silently awaiting the clarion call of destiny.

It is rare for a Tomb World to awaken to full function swiftly. With but the slightest flaw in the revivification cycle, the engrammic pathway of a sleeper scatters and degrades. In most cases, these coalesce over time to restore identity and purpose, but it is a process that can take decades, or even centuries, and cannot be hurried. Sometimes recovery never occurs and the sleeper is doomed forever to a mindless state.

There are thousands of Tomb Worlds scattered throughout the galaxy whose halls are thronged with shambling automatons, Necrons whose minds fled during hibernation, and whose bodies have been co-opted by a Tomb World's master program in an attempt to bring some form of order to their existence. Other Necrons refer to such places as the Severed Worlds, and they loathe and fear their inhabitants in equal measure. None of this is to say that even an individual lucky enough to achieve a flawless revivification awakens alert and aware.

One of the hidden tyrannies of biotransference was how it entrenched the gulf between the rulers and the ruled, for there were not resources enough to provide all Necrontyr with bodies capable of retaining the full gamut of personality and awareness. Thus, as was ever the case, the very finest bodies went to individuals of high rank: the Phaerons and Overlords, their Crypteks and nemesors. For the professional soldiery, the merely adequate was deemed appropriate. As for the common people, they received that which remained: comparatively crude bodies that were little more than lobotomised prisons. Numb to all joy and experience, they are bound solely to the will of their betters, their function meaningless without constant direction. Yet even here a tiny spark of self-awareness remains, enough only to torment the Necron with memories and echoes of the past it once knew. For these tortured creatures, death would be far preferable but, alas, they no longer have the wit to realise it.

DOLMEN GATES

In the closing years of the War in Heaven, the tides began to shift when the Necrons finally gained access to the webway. The C'tan known as Nyadra'zatha, the Burning One, had long desired to carry his eldritch fires into that space beyond space, and so showed the Necrons how to breach its boundaries. Through a series of living stone portals known as the Dolmen Gates, the Necrons were finally able to turn the Old Ones' greatest weapon against them, vastly accelerating the end of the War in Heaven.

The portals offered by the Dolmen Gates are neither so stable, nor so controllable as the naturally occurring entrances to the webway. Indeed, in some curious fashion, the webway can detect when its environs have been breached by a Dolmen Gate and swiftly attempts to seal off the infected spur until the danger has passed. So, Necrons entering the webway must reach their destination quickly, lest the network itself bring about their destruction.

Aeons have passed since those times. The Old Ones are gone, and the webway itself has become a tangled and broken labyrinth. Many Dolmen Gates were lost or abandoned during the time of the Great Sleep, and many more were destroyed by the Eldar. Those that remain grant access to but a small portion of the webway, much of that voluntarily sealed off by the Eldar to prevent further contamination. Yet the webway is immeasurably vast, and even these sundered skeins allow the Necrons a mode of travel that far outpaces those of the younger races. It is well that this is so. As a race bereft of psykers, the Necrons are incapable of Warp travel, and without access to the webway, they would be forced to rely once more on slow-voyaging stasis-ships, dooming them to isolation.

UNSLEEPING DEFENCES

A Tomb World is at its most vulnerable during the revivification process. The colossal amounts of energy generated are detectable across great distances, and are an irresistible lure to the inquisitive and acquisitive alike. In these early stages, it is unlikely that the army of a Tomb World proper will have awoken to full function, so defence lies in the hands of the Necrons' servitor robots – the Canoptek Spyders, Scarabs and Wraiths. Initially, these defenders will be directed by the Tomb World's master program, whose complex decision matrix allows it to calculate an efficient response to any perceived threat. As the threat level rises, so too does the intensity of the master program's counter-measures, prioritising the activation of the Tomb World's defences and the revivification of its armies according to the situation at hand. If all goes well, the master program's actions will be sufficient to drive out the invader, or at least stall their ingress until the first legions have awoken – at which point the master program surrenders command to the Tomb World's nobles.

When a large population centre of a younger race has evolved or expanded close to a Tomb World, the encoded programming delves deep into its archives and armouries in order to conduct an aggressive defence. Such Tomb Worlds are the ones that have expanded their spheres of influence most rapidly, for its rulers have awakened to find their full military might already mobilised and awaiting command. Indeed, the speed with which many Tomb Worlds of the Sautekh Dynasty have recovered lost territory is chiefly attributable to the (ultimately doomed) wave of Uluméathi colonies established on their coreworlds during late M39.

A RETURN TO POWER

To external observers, the behaviour of awoken Tomb Worlds must seem eclectic almost to the point of randomness. Some Necron Lords send diplomatic emissaries to other worlds, negotiating for the return of lost territories and artefacts, or cast off into the stars, searching for distant Tomb Worlds not yet awoken. Others focus attention inwards, avoiding unnecessary conflict with alien races to pursue internal politics or oversee the rebuilding of their planet to glory.

The vast majority of Tomb Worlds, however, take a more aggressive tack, launching resource raids, planetary invasions or full-blown genocidal purges. Yet even here, it is impossible to predict the precise form these deeds will take. Sometimes the Necrons attack in the full panoply and spectacle of honourable war, rigorously applying their ancient codes of battle. At others, every possible underhanded tactic is employed, from piracy and deception, to assassination and subornation. On other occasions, the campaign is less a martial action than a systematic extermination, the swatting of lesser life forms as they themselves would swat insects.

All of these acts, diverse though they are in scope and method, are directed towards a single common goal: the restoration of the Necron dynasties. Yet, with the Triarch long gone and huge numbers of Tomb Worlds lying desolate or dormant, there can be no galaxy-wide coordination, no grand strategy that will bring about Necron ascendancy. Instead, each Tomb World's ruler must fend for himself, pursuing whatever course he deems most suited to circumstance. For some, this is the domination of nearby threats and the sowing of terror on alien worlds. For others, it might be the recovery of cultural treasures, the stockpiling of raw materials for campaigns yet to come, or even the search for an organic species whose bodies might be suitable vessels for Necron minds, thus finally ending the curse of biotransference. Indeed, this last matter – the apotheosis from machine to living being – is the key motivating factor for many Necron nobles, for its possibility weighed heavily on the Silent King's mind at the moment of his final command.

All this is further complicated by the fact that the departure of the Silent King and the dissolution of the Triarch left no clear succession. As a result, the rulers of many Tomb Worlds see an opportunity not only to restore the dynasties of old, but also to improve their standing within the galaxy-wide Necron hierarchy. The motives of Necron nobles are often muddied by the pursuit of personal power, making accurate divination of an individual's intentions – and therefore of the campaigns conducted by his legions – nigh impossible.

> 'Adversary, know that your squalid colony rests upon a rightful crownworld of the Novokh Dynasty. Know also that whilst your presence cannot be tolerated, we are bound by code of honour to allow you opportunity to withdraw. You are therefore granted one solar month, commencing at termination of this transmission, to remove all trace of your presence. If you fail to accept this generous offer, my armies shall conclude these negotiations. We advise you not to mistake honourable warning for lack of resolve.'
>
> - Ultimatum received by Governor Mendican Harrow of hive world Dhol VI.

NECRON DYNASTIES

Even in life, the Necrontyr civilisation was one of strict protocol and process, governed by nobles whose rule was absolute. This rigid hierarchy became more entrenched during the transition from flesh to machine, and the awakening Necron civilisation is far more complex and stratified than the one that once ruled the galaxy.

Every Necron belongs to a royal dynasty, one of the great houses of the ancient Necrontyr. Allegiance to a dynasty was once purely a matter of family and tradition, but it is now entrenched through conquest and programming. Every Necron noble is truly individualistic and, whilst they might share a common set of customs and loyalties, they rarely have a unity of purpose beyond that imposed by their superiors. Accordingly, whilst several neighbouring worlds might owe allegiance to the same royal dynasty, the agendas they pursue depends entirely on the whims and goals of each Overlord or Lord, rather than the broader traditions of the dynasty.

Before the coming of the C'tan, there were many hundreds of Necrontyr dynasties. Some wielded vast political and military power while others were vestigial and broken, echoes of once great houses. Through the Wars of Secession, the rebellion against biotransference, the War in Heaven and the Great Sleep, many thousands of royal dynasties were destroyed. It is impossible to say how many survived, save that they number in the hundreds, or possibly thousands. Those dynasties listed here can be considered the most powerful of those that remain.

In the times before biotransference, the **Sautekh Dynasty** was ranked third most powerful of all the royal dynasties. Through chance or design, many of the Sautekh coreworlds survived the aeons better than other those of other dynasties. Now, this dynasty is more powerful than any other, and its nobility the most aggressive in attempting a new wave of expansion.

Much of the territory once ruled by the **Charnovokh Dynasty** lies far to the galactic southeast. Many of its dormant Tomb Worlds were devoured by Hive Fleet Behemoth, and countless others have been ravaged during the Imperium's counterattacks against the Tyranids. As a result, the remaining systems of the Charnovokh Dynasty are many, but small and scattered.

The worlds ruled by the **Oroskh Dynasty** are heavily infected by the flayer virus – the result of a deliberate contamination conducted by Pathfinders from the Alaitoc Craftworld. Year by year, the Oroskh Tomb Worlds' populations shrink further as ever more Necrons devolve into Flayed Ones.

The **Atun Dynasty** rules many Tomb Worlds on the northern galactic rim – the birthplace of the Necrontyr. Many of the ancient wonders of the galaxy lie under the control of the Phaeron of Atun and his powerful Overlords, and still many more wait to be uncovered from Tomb Worlds not yet awoken.

During the Wars of Secession, the nobles of the **Nekthyst Dynasty** earned themselves a reputation as turncoats and betrayers, for many of them held to pacts and alliances only so long as it served their interests. Though these events were long ago, the taint of dishonour still hangs heavy over the Nekthyst Dynasty, and few Phaerons of other lineages will stoop even to treat with them, let alone trust them.

The **Ogdobekh Dynasty** was ever famed for its technical mastery. As a result, its Tomb Worlds were more prepared for the Great Sleep, and more completely outfitted with backup systems. The dynasty's relative power is therefore greater than in ancient times, for its people have emerged far more reliably from hibernation than most.

The nobles of the **Oruscar Dynasty** were ever bitter rivals with those of the Sautekh Dynasty. Whilst the power of Sautekh was spread wide throughout the stars, Oruscar's holdings were limited to a handful of hallowed ancestral worlds laden with technological wonders. This rivalry is not ended, merely dormant. Both dynasties are, thus far, pursuing the wider goal of reclaiming the galaxy – but such a state of affairs is unlikely to last forever.

The territories of the **Nihilakh Dynasty** are parochial in the extreme, venturing little outside their domains. Whilst this isolationism is perhaps a boon to those alien races that dwell near to awakened Nihilakh Tomb Worlds, it also carries significant peril. Undepleted by the grind of military expansion, the armies of Nihilakh stand ready to take vengeance on any interloper. If attacked, the Nihilakh do not rest until the aggressor has been utterly destroyed.

RULERS OF THE NECRONS

Highest of the Necron nobles are the Phaerons, the rulers of entire dynasties including many planetary systems. Beneath these are the Overlords, who rule clusters of Tomb Worlds within their Phaeron's domain. Lower still are the Lords, each charged with the keeping of a single core or fringeworld. So deeply are these titles mired in tradition that they are universally constant. However, the titles of subordinate nobles and functionaries, which make up advisory councils and specialist convocations, are subject to almost infinite variety.

Gravs, vymarks and thantars are but a few of the titles given to lower tier nobles; almost identical in terms of rank and responsibility, the only real difference arises from which dynasty the individual hails from. Many Necron titles are hereditary, dating to the earliest days of the Necrontyr – some were relatively late inventions, crafted as a means by which nobles of lesser rank could be rewarded for their service. As the sphere of Necrontyr dominion expanded ever further, the scope and application of titles passed far beyond any form of central control. Each royal dynasty created ever more elaborate titles based on its own traditions as a means of self-justification. Like many civilisations, the more grandiose or long-winded the title, the more likely it was merely an attempt to disguise low status.

This tanglework becomes particularly byzantine when a Phaeron from one royal dynasty gains sway over a world from another. The resulting protocol is tedious beyond the endurance of living creatures, but for the Necron nobility it is merely another way of whiling away eternity. To make matters worse, if a Phaeron is deposed or destroyed, his replacement will sometimes insist that all existing ranks be amended to reflect the traditions of his own house. To take such a step, the incumbent must be entirely sure of his position, as a challenge to tradition is sure to rouse discontent within his own court.

The ranking structures within the Necrontyr armies and fleets have remained constant, no matter how vast and disparate the dynasties have become. For example, every time any Necrons go to war, the title of nemesor is bestowed upon the overall commander of the battlefield. This allows armies from across the stars to join forces, even if they have never met, and suffer no decrease in efficiency. This entrenched command structure helped ease the transition of Imotekh the Stormlord from nemesor to Phaeron of the Sautekh Dynasty.

THE ROYAL COURTS

Every Phaeron and Overlord is served by a Royal Court, which assists in the administration of Tomb Worlds and the execution of military campaigns. A Royal Court consists of a group of Lords, Crypteks, and in the courts of Phaerons, Overlords, who owe fealty through oath or family bonds. Though flesh is long since a memory for the Necrons, ties of blood remain as important as they ever were. Each Lord will also be served by their own lesser courts. Only nobles of the very lowest ranks do not have courts of their own, yet even these mimic their betters by keeping a circle of untitled advisors from the most acceptably sentient of their vassals. Of course, given the paucity of wit in such advisors, these courts are but shadowed mockeries of the real things. However, in the ongoing battle for status and proper protocol, even a laughable court is considered better than no court at all.

THE NECRON LEGIONS

The size of a Royal Court is not only important in terms of political status and prestige; it also determines a noble's military status. The larger the Royal Court, the greater his seniority and the more troops under his command. Even a noble who lacks for a Royal Court commands a legion of Necron Warriors, a few phalanxes of Immortals and Deathmarks, as well as a phalanx of Lychguard. Added to this are forces not aligned to any particular dynasty. Triarch Praetorians, the surviving agents of the vanished Triarch, fight alongside any nemesor whom they judge to have the best interests of the dynasties at heart. Nihilistic Destroyers can be lured to a battle with promises of carnage and slaughter, whilst Crypteks can be retained through acts of patronage. Few nobles, no matter how desperate their plight, deliberately seek the aid of the devolved Flayed Ones, although as these charnel creatures inevitably turn up to battles of their own accord, this reluctance is of little account.

The more senior a noble's position in the hierarchy, the greater the number and quality of the troops he has authority over. Furthermore, a ranking noble also has indirect command over all the forces controlled by the members of his Royal Court, who, in turn, have authority over the forces controlled by their subordinates, and so on. As even the smallest of Tomb Worlds has at least two-score nobles of lesser rank, an Overlord can commonly draw upon at least a hundred legions of Necron Warriors, should he have need.

> 'What care I that my legions are faceless? Identity matters only to those who have the ability to think: my Immortals and Lychguard, perhaps; my Lords and Crypteks, certainly. For the remainder of my vassals? Well, suffice to say that the concept of glory is wasted on the inglorious.'
>
> *- Imotekh the Stormlord*
> *Phaeron of the Sautekh Dynasty*
> *Regent of Mandragora*

DYNASTIC GLYPHS

All Necrons, noble and common-born, are bound together by the symbol of the ancient Necrontyr dynasties, the Ankh of the Triarch. Each of the royal dynasties also has its own glyph, the designs of which have remained unchanged over the aeons. Nobles bear the dynasty's mark, normally upon a death mask, a cloak or sometimes as a stylised detail on weaponry or tokens of office. The most arrogant of nobles bear a glyph upon their breastplate in place of the Ankh of the Triarch, though to do so is to defy tradition and protocol.

Only nobles of the highest rank are permitted to bear their dynasty's glyph in its fullest form. Those of lesser rank bear only elements of the glyph, symbolising their position relative to a royal dynasty's heart of power. A handful of nobles do not bear a glyph at all – some hail from royal dynasties destroyed during the War in Heaven, while others were stripped of rank and status for some long ago transgression. In either event, such a noble is considered untrustworthy at best, with treachery either in his past or in his future.

Dynastic glyphs are unique to nobles. The common soldiery, such as Necron Warriors and Immortals, are largely considered to be interchangeable chattel. As such, they are thought unworthy of direct association with the proud lineage of a particular dynasty – although the colours of their death masks and armour sometimes echo ancient heraldry and thus indirectly reflect their allegiance. In contrast, war engines, such as Monoliths and Doomsday Arks, are often marked with dynastic glyphs – they are considered to be the personal weaponry of a particular noble and therefore warrant a higher status than even the Necron Warriors that crew them.

THE FALL OF THE KHANSU DYNASTY

By no means did all of the Necrontyr people go willingly to the chambers of transformation, but the nobility of the Khansu Dynasty fought the onset of biotransference more than most, and at every turn. When it became clear that no amount of political manoeuvring or manipulation could prevent what was to come, the Khansu Dynasty fought in armed revolt. Yet one Phaeron, no matter how powerful, could not hope to fight the rest of the dynasties and their C'tan masters. Ascendant Prince Rakszan was one of the few amongst the Khansu Dynasty to choose biotransference of his own volition, and he cursed his people for their foolishness in resisting what could only be a new age of glory. For his loyalty, Rakszan was granted high military rank and his first campaigns were those that brought his rebellious kinsmen to heel. One by one, Khansu's coreworlds fell, the crownworld of Hamûn last of all, and those few rebels that survived were dragged to the chambers of transformation.

At first, Rakszan was pleased, for his people would now have the chance to regain honour lost in revolt. Yet, as the War in Heaven ground on, he witnessed the C'tan and their underlings systematically destroying his dynasty. Indignity was added to defeat, with the Necrons of the Khansu Dynasty deployed at the forefront of every battle, or else despatched on campaigns where there was little hope of success and none of survival. Little by little, Rakszan came to realise the terrible depths of his mistake. When the rebellion against the C'tan began, none fought so hard as he to see the star-gods toppled.

By this time, the Khansu Dynasty was lost forever, its nobles destroyed in the War in Heaven, its Warriors and Immortals seized by other dynasties and reprogrammed to their service. In all the galaxy, only Rakszan remained to speak for his slaughtered kin, and he held himself a traitor to their memory. With no other way remaining to atone for his betrayal, Rakszan swore that he would see every surviving fragment of every C'tan caged, so that they could never again arise. It is a quest that continues to this day...

THE SAUTEKH DYNASTY

Royal hierarchy, circa 998.M41. Note that only the top tiers are shown.
Several tiers of the court structure exist below the lowest level shown here.

Orikan the Diviner
Astromancer to the Royal Court

Navgran the Eternal
High Transmuter and Omnimutander

Judicator Battalions of the Triarch Praetorians

Overseer Ogdra
Architect of Doom

Imotekh the Stormlord
Phaeron of the Sautekh Dynasty
Regent of Mandragora

Lord High Judicator Krammathal
Enforcer of the Codes of Battle

Vargard Osirok
Bodyguard to the Phaeron

Lord Koszvar
Dictator of Santar

Overseer Kadgakh
Court Magister

Overseer Djedrym
Court Obliterator

Overlord Ogdovakh
Overlord of the Sautekh Fringeworlds
Regent of Vanur

Lord Valgekh
Despoiler of V'nox

Nemesor Zahndrekh
Overlord of the Sautekh Coreworlds
Regent of Gidrim

Destroyer Cults of the Red Harvest

Vargard Obyron
Bodyguard to the Nemesor

Lord Azdrakh
Ruler of Ghor

The Corpse Lord
Vycount of the Blood Palace

Flayed One Pack of the Blood Palace

Executioner Ezandrakh
Nomarch of Sr'byna

Lord Zendrik
Ruler of Novokor

Lord Trabant
Nomarch of Gintarro

Lord Kastivhor
Nomarch of Ystarkh

Overlord Szaron
Regent of Somonor

Lord Azgorekh
Ruler of Jorokh

Overlord Naszar
Regent of Gheisten

Overseer Zerikyn
Chronostatistician

Overseer Zamar
High Zephyrist

Lord Zamanog
Chamberlain of the Royal Court of Gheisten

Gravs of the Nemesor's Royal Court

Gravs of the Ghorric Court

Thantars of the Gheisten Royal Court

Gravs of the Novokoric Court

Edictrons of the Ystarkhan Court

THE CLIENT DYNASTY OF SEKEMTAR
Conquered by Imotekh during the Wars of Secession

THE CLIENT DYNASTY OF ARRYNMAROK
Swore allegiance to Imotekh circa 798 M41.

NECRON TOMB WORLDS

For many of the galaxy's myriad races, the re-emergent Necrons are but one terror amongst many in the darkness. Even within the Imperium, the Necrons are only dimly understood, with just a handful of individuals aware of the true scale of their threat.

Just as Necron society is rigidly tiered, so too are its Tomb Worlds. The most important are the crownworlds, oldest and proudest of all the Necron planets and the sites from which dynasties and planetary clusters are governed. Crownworlds were once hubs of galactic power, buttressed by tithe and tribute sent from elsewhere within their dynasties. With access to such great resource-wealth, crownworlds were able to construct the most reliable stasis-crypts. As a result, crownworld inhabitants that have weathered the slumbering millennia, without falling foul of external circumstance, have done so in excellent condition – though this only deepens the tragedy when a crownworld is lost to galactic calamity.

Next in importance are coreworlds, planets which together form the heart of a dynasty. The rulers of coreworlds would inevitably be close kin to the regent of their crownworld, ensuring a bond of dynastic loyalty endured between the often diverse planets. Though neither so majestic nor so mighty as crownworlds, the coreworlds were great powers to be reckoned with in their heyday and, barring disaster, are so again in the 41st Millennium.

Finally, fringeworlds are planets of tertiary importance, not viewed as being of high enough status to be numbered amongst a dynasty's coreworlds. Fringeworlds were often poor or distant colonies, able to contribute to the wider realm only in terms of manual labour or as a location for penal institutions. Some fringeworlds will once have counted amongst the coreworlds of a different dynasty, but have since been conquered or otherwise subsumed into the dominion of their current ruler, thus descending in status.

PLACES OF POWER

There is no such thing as a 'typical' Tomb World. Each answers only to the will of its ruler, and thus his proclivities define everything from its grand campaigns to trivialities such as architectural styles and forms of address between ranks. Nevertheless, there is one common cause that binds all: the rebuilding of the dynasties of old, and the return of the Necrons to their rightful supremacy over the ignorant galaxy.

MANDRAGORA THE GOLDEN, CROWNWORLD OF THE SAUTEKH DYNASTY

Mandragora was always an important world, a hub for the Necron armies that did battle on the eastern rim of the galaxy. When the War in Heaven ended, Mandragora's stasis-crypts were filled to capacity with some of the finest warriors that the Necron dynasties could command. Mandragora's defences were second to none, as befitted a world of its status, and it survived the Great Sleep intact and safe from the attentions of plunderers.

So did Mandragora emerge from hibernation not only hale and whole, but with vast legions at its command – a situation its new Phaeron, Imotekh the Stormlord, was quick to exploit. Ordering Mandragora's Dolmen Gates reactivated,

he sent forces to seize the many coreworlds from the Ork hordes of Warboss Snagratoof. With the Orks driven off or destroyed, the reclaimed Tomb Worlds were then awoken, swelling Imotekh's forces further. Since then, the armies of Mandragora have proved an ever-present threat on the Imperium's eastern borders, and one that continues to grow.

GHEDEN, PLANET OF SHADOW, CROWNWORLD OF THE NIHILAKH DYNASTY

Due to a devastating fault in a dimensional stabiliser array, the crownworld of Gheden is half-phased into a pocket dimension for all but a few hours of its stellar orbit. What was first thought of as a catastrophe has since proved to be a great boon to the Necrons of Gheden, as their world is now almost entirely impervious to assault. Deep beneath Gheden's surface lies the Oracle Chamber, wherein the bulbous head of an ancient alien prophet is kept alive through a combination of stasis fields and temporal stabilisers. The prophet's thoughts are projected as multifaceted holographic images which, in theory, show events yet to unfurl. That said, the creature continually rails against his ghoulish imprisonment and obfuscates the images so that they mislead as often as they are truthful.

ANCIENT ENEMIES

Of all the galaxy's major powers, only the Eldar see the Necrons for the threat they truly are — and even they cannot be sure how many Tomb Worlds slumber in the darkness. After the War in Heaven, the Eldar took up a silent watch for any sign of Necron re-emergence, and set watch on worlds they suspected of nurturing hidden tombs. Many such worlds were seeded with life and adopted as homes by outcasts and Exodites, whose descendants would maintain the vigil. Where this was not possible, suspected Tomb Worlds were marked on a great crystal map so that their locations would not be lost. Yet as time passed, the Eldar became distracted by their own plights and thus forgot their sworn duty. By the time of the Fall — the terrible birth of Slaanesh — the slumbering Necrons had been all but forgotten. Only in the Black Library and amongst a few outspoken segments of Eldar society did the vigil continue.

For the Eldar, the Necrons are a nightmare come to life. The children of Isha hold soullessness to be the very worst of all fates, and the Necrons therefore provoke an abiding terror that the Eldar can never truly suppress. For the Seer Council of the Alaitoc Craftworld, however, a time of terrible vindication is at hand. The Eldar of Alaitoc remembered whilst their peers forgot. They recovered the fragments of the great map, spread their networks of outcasts and Exodites ever wider and waited for the ancient enemy to return. So it is that whilst most craftworlds are re-honing half remembered strategies, Alaitoc is reaching its hand, assailing the Necrons on their own territory, sabotaging their Tomb Worlds and embattling their legions whenever the opportunity permits.

THANATOS AND THE CELESTIAL ORRERY

The Tomb World of Thanatos is a hollow planet, and hidden at its heart is one of the galaxy's greatest treasures – the Celestial Orrery. Crafted by artisans of the Oruscar Dynasty long before the onset of the War in Heaven, this web of hologram and living metal is beyond price for its artistic value alone. Yet the Celestial Orrery is far more than mere decorative finery. The tiny pinpricks of glowing light suspended within the impossibly intricate matrix record the positions of every star in the galaxy. Snuff out one of these lights and its physical counterpart will go supernova long millennia before its destined time, bringing fiery oblivion to all nearby worlds.

Such an act cannot be performed without consideration, however, as each star destroyed in this fashion upsets the fundamental forces of the galaxy, setting off a catastrophic chain reaction. Only with further manipulation of the Celestial Orrery can these forces be returned to their proper balance, and this invariably takes many thousands of years of constant and precise micromanagement.

With so much power at their fingertips, it is well that the Royal Court of Thanatos is not given to maniacal displays. Rather, they see themselves as gardeners of creation and dispassionately use the Orrery in a precise and sparing manner, pruning the galaxy only out of need to prevent it from becoming wild and overgrown. Alas, this restraint is not something universally respected. Unending war rages across Thanatos' barren continents and in the skies above, as the armies and fleets of the Oruscar Dynasty strive to prevent the Celestial Orrery from falling into the incautious hands of aliens and other Necrons alike.

THE BONE KINGDOM OF DRAZAK

In the extreme northeast of the galaxy lie the Ghoul Stars. Here, on worlds lit by the cold rays of dying suns, tread creatures out of primal nightmare: Cythor Fiends, Togoran Bloodreeks and other creatures so alien as to seem born out of the supernatural. Yet even here, one horror outpaces all others – the Bone Kingdom of Drazak.

Drazak is a haunt of Flayed Ones, those cursed Necrons blighted by a hunger for flesh. They stalk through Drazak's desolate streets, fighting over gobbets of rotting meat and shards of bone, desperate to sate the clamour of their deluded senses. Only one amongst Drazak's entire population is proof from its pervading madness – Valgûl, the Fallen Lord. From his throne of splintered bone and tanned skin, Valgûl rules over this charnel kingdom, his one good eye ever fixed upon retaining what small measure of order he can. Seemingly, Valgûl remains untouched by the flayer virus that has consumed his people, but what truly sane creature would willingly live amongst gibbering Flayed Ones? Perhaps he remains from a sense of duty, or maybe his personal madness merely takes another, more subtle, form.

Valgûl's rule is not founded on reason – the devolved nature of his subjects makes such notions laughable – but is grounded in his ability to provide the gory bounty in which his subjects delight. Every few solar months, when no more meat remains – whether because it has been torn into fragments too tiny to scrabble over or simply due to inexorable rot – Valgûl announces a new Time of Bounty, and despatches the fleets of Drazak to raid nearby worlds. These reavers of Drazak seek not riches nor conventional plunder – only tithes of gore and cooling blood.

TRANTIS, THE RAIDER'S MOON

Though nominally a Tomb World, Trantis is, in truth, but a fringeworld, and satellite of the much larger and resource-rich Imperial world of Mandal. Since revival, the Necrons of Trantis have been a terror on Mandal's farming and mining communities. Striking always in the hours of darkness, low-flying squadrons of Night Scythes flit over the landscape, deploying small forces of raiders to plunder and pillage.

It is not uncommon for entire settlements to be overwhelmed and harvested within a single night with only a large and barren crater to show where people once lived and worked. Mandal's communes are so far apart that whole days can pass before a disappearance is noted, and certainly too distant for help to be dispatched once a raid begins. The inhabitants have thus learnt to dread the onset of dusk. As darkness descends, curfew begins, blast doors are sealed and sentries set. Yet every few nights another settlement vanishes without warning and without trace.

Ironically, Trantis was only ever intended as a way station for resources and raw materials. It lacks the ability to use more than a fraction of the plunder from the planet below and was to ship the excess to other nearby coreworlds. Since the Great Sleep, however, Trantis' portion of the webway has become sundered from all others, effectively isolating it from those worlds it used to supply. Accordingly, Trantis is slowly drowning in plundered resources for which it has little use. Yet still the raids continue...

ZAPENNEC, THE REAVEWORLD

In the final hours of the War in Heaven, one of its greatest battles occurred above Zapennec, crownworld of the Sarnekh Dynasty. There, Zapennec's royal fleet fought valiantly to repel an Eldar assault of almost incalculable size. The battle was a brief one, but no less deadly for all that. Whilst the surviving Eldar retreated, leaving the planet itself unharmed, its orbit was, from that moment, clogged with the spiralling and blackened wreckage of the once-proud fleets. So soon after the battle did the Great Sleep descend, that the Necrons of Zapennec had no time to clear their skies. Thus did they enter hibernation with their planet shielded by a spinning shroud of wraithbone and living metal.

So would things remain until late M41 and the return of the Sarnekh Dynasty's most notorious outcast, the self-styled pirate king, Thaszar the Invincible. Awakening on Athonos, the world to which he had been exiled, and driven by some urge he could not identify, Thaszar returned to Zapennec. Finding it deep in hibernation, he inveigled his way into the Tomb World's master program. In short order he convinced the master program that he, Thaszar the Invincible, was no dishonoured exile, but in fact the rightful Phaeron. For good measure, he then ordered that this updated status be encoded into the minds of the Tomb World's slumbering Necrons. So did the outcast of Zapennec become its ruler, and those who had banished him became his servants.

Under Thaszar's command, the ancient and noble crownworld of the Sarnekh Dynasty has been made over into the Reaveworld. In the shroud of wreckage, Thaszar has access to all the raw materials he will ever need to build a pirate fleet the scale of which has not been seen for a million years; in the reprogrammed Necrons of Zapennec, he has crews and captains of unfailing loyalty. Thaszar's vessels have already begun to prowl both the webway and realspace, and the galaxy will surely come to rue the day he reawakened.

THE EMPIRE OF THE SEVERED

When radiation storms ravaged the Tomb World of Sarkon, they destroyed forever the memory engrams of every Necron interred therein. With its charges thus rendered mindless, the complex's master program took charge of their bodies. Little realising its own systems had also been damaged, the master program observed the quiet order it had brought to Sarkon and resolved to carry it far and wide. Searching its records, the master program sent its mindless legions to invade Takarak, a slumbering Tomb World located nearby. Takarak's defences were swiftly overwhelmed, and the Sarkoni Emperor (for thus was how the master program now thought of itself) erased the minds of Takarak's inhabitants and claimed their bodies for itself. As of 967.M41, another three Tomb Worlds have been overcome in this manner, and the Sarkoni Emperor has begun to extend its will across other, non-Necron worlds, using mindshackle scarabs to bring any unruly living creatures under its direct control.

MOEBIUS, THE TWISTED CATACOMB, CROWNWORLD OF THE NEKTHYST DYNASTY

The nobles of the Nekthyst Dynasty ever had a talent for deception, and their crownworld stands as an enduring testament to that devious mindset. The hyperspace corridors connecting Moebius' countless crypts take the form of an ever-shifting maze, ensuring that no journey through the catacombs is ever the same twice – as at least one Deathwatch kill-team has found out to its cost.

THE STASIS DOCKS OF SEIDON

In ancient times, Seidon lay at the heart of Necrontyr expansion. It was from this coreworld's stardocks that the torch-ships set out into the stars, carrying colonists beyond the boundaries of Necrontyr space. Throughout the War in Heaven, the wharves of Seidon continued to ply their trade, but instead sent expeditionary forces in search of fresh worlds to conquer. Every thirty-three weeks, another vast stasis-ship would launch from the dockyards of Seidon, carrying a legion of Immortals to some distant planet.

When the Great Sleep ended and Seidon woke once again to full function, its rulers decided that they could best serve their final orders by continuing in their mission of conquest. Alas, unbeknownst to the Tomb World's Overlord, Seidon's master program suffered corruption during the Great Sleep and many records were destroyed or inexplicably altered. No longer are the great ships set forth on courses that intersect with planetary systems. Instead, each vessel is launched on a random heading, as likely to plunge it into the blazing heart of a star or into the tendrilled maw of a Tyranid Hive Fleet as it is to result in safe planetfall. Yet as Seidon's nobility have no need to query the master program, the fault continues to go unnoticed. Thus, for every thirty-three weeks that pass, another legion of Immortals depart on their perilous journey into the unknown...

'Order. Unity. Obedience. We taught the galaxy these things long ago, and we will do so again.'
- Imotekh the Stormlord

TRAKONN OF TEN THOUSAND SPIRES, CROWNWORLD OF THE DYVANAKH DYNASTY

The Necrons of Trakonn originally awoke in early M41, but were not to shake off their hibernation-induced disorientation for nearly five hundred years. This proved sufficient time for their Tomb World to draw the attention of a neighbouring forge world, and the internal battle to regain consciousness swiftly overlapped with a series of wars against the Imperium.

Now the siege has finally ended, and Trakonn's armies have finally cast the upstart humans from their planet and begun the search for the other Tomb Worlds of their dynasty. Alas, they have been unable to make contact with even a single one, and must now assume that the records of old no longer match the reality of the modern galaxy. In this they are, at best, tangentially correct. The missing Dyvanakh Tomb Worlds were actually engulfed and destroyed by a Warp storm thousands of years before Trakonn emerged from slumber. Ignorant of this fact, the nobles of Trakonn continue their hopeless search to this day.

THE BLOOD VATS OF ZANTRAGORA

The nobles of Zantragora have but one overriding goal. Their aim is apotheosis, the undoing of biotransference's curse by transferring their consciousnesses into the bodies of other sentient creatures. Their belief that such a thing is possible is rooted both in the final command of the Silent King, and in prophecies made at the time of the Great Sleep. These, while predicting that apotheosis would come to pass, lacked much in the way of detail, and it has ever been unclear whether the Necrons need to take over other bodies, or clone new ones for their eternal minds to inhabit.

To this end, the legions and fleets of Zantragora scour the galaxy for fresh subjects, following strict search patterns lest they somehow miss a world whose inhabitants hold the key. Hundreds of thousands of samples, both living and dead, are taken from every planet in the search pattern. Sealed in stasis-sleep, these are conveyed back to Zantragora to feed the never-ending series of autopsies, gene-splicing, tissue mutation and molecular deconstruction that typifies the quest for apotheosis. Progress is excruciatingly slow, and every step is marked in the blood of lesser species.

TOMB WORLDS BEYOND NUMBER

These Tomb Worlds represent no more than a handful of the many millions spread throughout the galaxy. Each revived world has its own idiosyncrasies, and the number is ever growing. Who can say how many far-flung outposts of Man have their foundations set upon a planet long ago claimed by an immeasurably older civilisation, inhabitants blissfully unaware of the slumbering horror at their planet's core.

In these days of reawakening, no world can rest easy...

RISE OF THE NECRONS

As yet, but a fraction of the galaxy's worlds have fallen under the Necrons' creeping shadow but, as their influence grows, so too does the scope of their campaigns. Whether the danger comes from a long-dead tomb buried beneath a planet's surface, or from the marauding fleets and armies of awakening dynasties finally stretching forth the might of old, there is but one truth: nowhere is safe.

THE SANDS OF FORDRIS

Warboss Skullkrak had led his boyz to the ghost world of Fordris pursuing rumours of ancient weaponry. He'd been hoping such tools could tip the balance in his campaign against the Raven Guard's 3rd Company, but after weeks of searching, all he'd discovered was that Fordris' seas were highly acidic and that its sand got *everywhere*.

Yet Fordris was neither lifeless nor uninhabited, as Skullkrak discovered when the first wave of Necron Warriors emerged from the blood-red seas. Brackish water streaming from their bodies, the soulless androids strode across the obsidian sands, each marching in perfect unison with every other, save for where circuitry misfires caused an involuntary twitch or stumble. Then, as Skullkrak bawled and bellowed his lads to 'get 'em, ya slugz' the Necron phalanx came to an abrupt halt, swung their gauss flayers to bear, and the killing began.

The first volley cut deep into the disordered Orks. Skullkrak, being somewhat quicker-witted than his followers, survived by hoisting one of the lads off his feet to use as cover. As a second torrent of energy crackled into the greenskins, Skullkrak threw aside his erstwhile shield and roared at his boys once more. This time, the call of the Waaagh! was taken up across the length and breadth of the shoreline. Choppas flailing, the Orks hurled themselves into the storm of emerald energies. Such a charge would have been sufficient to freeze the blood of any mortal foe, but the Necrons were not so easily shaken. Three more volleys did the mechanical warriors fire, pitching dozens of greenskins into the sand – but then the Orks were upon them.

Skullkrak hurled himself bodily into the Necron ranks, swinging his massive war axe in a succession of brutal alloy-crunching arcs that smashed heads from shoulders, crushed rib cages and shattered limbs. Within moments the Ork Warboss stood alone in a sea of twisted metal, roaring his dominance. Yet Skullkrak's claim to victory was premature. Even as the last Necron fell, the regeneration circuits of the first triggered, drawing upon hidden power reserves to reknit broken limbs, repath critical circuits and return the warrior to full function. Thus, even before Skullkrak's jubilant shout had finished echoing off the cliffs, the Ork Warboss found himself surrounded once again by the reanimated forms of those he had hacked apart only moments before.

Such was the scene all across the shore. Again and again the Orks' ferocity bore Necron Warriors to the ground, but again and again the fallen dragged themselves back into the fight. Decapitated heads were reclaimed by grasping hands, and severed arms scrabbled across the sand in search of their sundered bodies. As the momentum of the Ork charge faded, the Necrons began to hold their own in the bitter battle. Still acting in unison, the Necron Warriors hacked at the Orks with heavy-bladed bayonets and, unlike their opponents, the greenskins that were struck down did not rise again. Only near to Skullkrak was the fight still in the Orks' favour, for the Warboss had taken to smashing his opponents into as many, and as small, pieces as possible to delay their inevitable reassembly.

So lost was he in the joy of battle that Skullkrak did not notice the swiftly rising tide until its ruddy waters were lapping at his feet. The dynamic of the battle changed as the sea rose up the beach to swallow the sands. For the first time since the fight had begun, downed Necrons were failing to regenerate, as vital components were swept out into the seething waters of the bay. Yet the rising tide also sucked at the Orks' feet, making footing treacherous. Worse, those Necrons that managed to repair did so hidden beneath the waves and many an Ork was dragged beneath the surface by grasping mechanical hands. Bellowing at his lads to follow, the Warboss ran back up the beach as swiftly as the drag of water about his legs would allow.

There, under the shadow of the cliff face, the Orks prepared to make their stand. The waters below were quieter now. Only a handful of Necrons were visible above the waves, and a handful of sustained volleys pitched them beneath the surface. The greenskins let out a cheer, but the raucous noise swiftly died away as, out in the bay, the waters parted once more and a slab-sided Monolith heaved its way to the surface. Gunfire scattering off its armoured flanks, the inexorable machine glided slowly towards Skullkrak and his remaining boys. There was an ear-splitting whine, the crystal atop the Monolith glowed a piercing white and then all that was left of the Orks was a pile of smouldering ash.

Far beneath the surface of the bay, in a vaulted stone chamber, two enthroned Necrons watched a holographic recreation of Skullkrak's demise. Rising, one banished the hologram with a dissatisfied wave of his hand. 'Combat efficiency remains at seventy percent of acceptable parameters. Further data is necessary to complete the required optimisation.'

'Indeed,' replied the other, also rising. 'Recommend activation of mindshackle cluster XD11101 – humans will provide a suitable comparator.' The first Necron nodded to indicate his assent and issued the necessary interstitial command. 'It is done. If the subject performs as expected, we have three months to prepare.'

Shortly thereafter, three sectors distant, Tech-Priest Dreicon Brudac began preparations to investigate a reported cache of xenos technology, located on an out-of-the-way world known as Fordris…

THE CONQUEST OF UTTU PRIME

Nemesor Zahndrekh's ultimatum had given the Imperial defenders of Uttu Prime one solar month to withdraw, as was required by the codes of battle. Yet, when the deadline had passed, the foolish humans had not availed themselves of this most generous of offers. Indeed, whilst the Necron fleet held in intentional abeyance in orbit around Uttu Prime's desert moon, four regiments of Catachan Jungle Fighters and three companies of Imperial Fists Space Marines had come to reinforce the contested world. So it was that when Zahndrekh finally launched his assault, he did so against a planet with formidable defences. However, when his courtiers argued against prosecuting the war to completion, the nemesor merely issued a grating laugh and sent the interstitial command that set his fleet in motion.

Zahndrekh initially ignored Uttu Prime's outlying cities, focussing his assault on Fort Anan, the planetary capital. Zahndrekh's first attack wave was a dozen squadrons of Doom Scythe fighter craft. They swarmed over Fort Anan's fortifications, death rays raising great furrows of twisted metal and stone as they ploughed through bastions, ferrocrete walls and the luckless defenders therein. To their credit, the humans put up a spirited resistance. Hydra Flak Tanks and defence lasers scoured the skies, driving off or blasting apart many of the Necron aircraft. Yet each time a Doom Scythe was destroyed, another immediately peeled off from the main group to exact vengeance. Soon, Fort Anan was stripped of aerial defences, and the landings began.

Transport craft followed in the wake of the first attack wave. Night Scythes flew low over the wreckage of crashed Necron flyers and Imperial bastions. Small arms fire scattered across the Night Scythes' armoured hulls as their flickering invasion beams delivered Zahndrekh's assault troops into the heart of the humans' defences. Phalanx upon phalanx of Immortals and Necron Warriors stalked through the fresh ruins, gauss weapons blazing in unnaturally precise volleys as they drove the Catachans back. Here and there, an officer's barked orders held the Guardsmen in line, but where those commanders fell, the Imperial lines went into full retreat.

It was as the attackers' lines reached the governor's citadel that the Imperial Fists finally made their presence known. Thunderhawk Gunships screamed through the skies, shredding the oncoming Necron Warriors with heavy bolter fire and blasting Immortals limb from limb with missile strikes. As the gunships touched down amongst the rubble to disgorge Space Marines into the fray, the Necrons shifted to defensive protocols and awaited reinforcements. Alas for the Imperial Fists; from his vantage point in orbit, Zahndrekh had marked the approach of the Thunderhawks long before they had made their presence known planet side. Thus, even as the roar of bolter-fire echoed through Fort Anan's ruins, a shadow fell over the battlefield as the Megalith descended.

The Megalith was no ordinary war engine, but a vast floating fortress. Green fire lanced out from its flanks, blasting Thunderhawks from the air or crippling them on the ground. As the shadow grew larger, chunks of the Megalith's under-structure broke away, the blocks falling lazily to the ground. They were no mere wreckage, but Monoliths detaching from the mother ship's hull. As each touched down, it added firepower to the barrage assailing the Imperial Fists.

The Space Marines must have determined that they were doomed, but duty and stubborn tenacity made them redouble their efforts. Lascannon and multi-melta fire flickered through the ruins, the beams converging to pierce the Monoliths' living metal hulls. Assault squads threw themselves at the Necron phalanxes, chainsword teeth screaming as they ripped through metal bodies. However, the Megalith was now close enough to the ground to bring its invasion beams into play. Ghoulish light flickered over the battlefield as teleport beams activated, delivering Doomsday Arks, legions of Necron Immortals, as well as Zahndrekh and his personal guard, into the thick of the battle.

Those Space Marines that yet survived now withdrew to the governor's citadel, but three Doomsday Arks converged their fire on the great adamantium gate. For a handful of moments it glowed an angry red, then burst into fragments with an ear-splitting crack. As the Imperial Fists fell back deeper into the citadel, Zahndrekh raised his warscythe in salute to the doomed foe. Then the scythe swept down and the nemesor led his army through the ruined gate. Shortly thereafter, Fort Anan had fallen. The rest of Uttu Prime would soon follow, and another world would be added to the territory of Gidrim.

'It is a source of constant consternation that my opponents cannot correlate their innate inferiority with their inevitable defeat. It would seem that stupidity is as eternal as war.'

- Nemesor Zahndrekh of the Sautekh Dynasty, Overlord of the Crownworld of Gidrim

THE SIEGE OF SOMONOR

When the Eldar Farseer Eldorath Starbane led his war host to the Tomb World of Somonor, he expected to face a Necron tomb disoriented from its long sleep. Yet such a simple battle was not to be. Imotekh the Stormlord, his campaign of reconquest ascendant after a series of pivotal victories against the Imperium of Man, had come to Somonor seeking to bend its Overlord to his will. The arrival of the Eldar had sped negotiations in Imotekh's favour, for Somonor could not stand against this ancient enemy alone. The Tomb World's stasis-crypts had been ill-prepared for the Great Sleep and many thousands of warriors had passed into dust; those that had survived were rising slowly and fitfully. Thusly, Somonor's Overlord Szaron had little hesitation in pledging allegiance to the growing Sautekh Dynasty, for the alternative was to see his domain destroyed at Starbane's hands. With the pact sealed, Imotekh's priorities swiftly turned to battle – a battle that would have to be won through guile as much as through force of arms.

THE WAR HOST STRIKES

So it was that when Eldorath Starbane led his advance force to the chill caldera that concealed the tomb's entrance, he found it held against him. Confident of victory, the Farseer launched his attack without waiting for the rest of the host – it was a mistake that would cost the Eldar dearly. For every advance the Eldar made, Imotekh had prepared a counter. Nowhere was this more clearly seen than when a Wave Serpent and its Vyper squadron escort split off from the main assault and dove hard towards the battle's heart, their goal to assail Imotekh directly. Yet Imotekh had expected such a move; indeed, he had left certain sectors of his defence enticingly weak to provoke such an attempt. So it was that as the Vypers closed into killing range, there was a blinding flash of emerald light, and the immovable bulk of a Monolith materialised between the Eldar and their prey. Unable to pull up in time, the lead Vyper slammed full-tilt into the slab-sided war vessel, the resulting fireball leaving not so much as a scorch mark on the Monolith. Saved by a split-second's warning and their pilots' preternatural reflexes, the other Vypers broke formation and banked hard, swarming about the Monolith's flanks like angry insects as they brought their weapons to bear on the new target. Yet the damage had already been done, and with the Vyper screen disrupted, the Monolith was free to bring its particle whip to bear on the Wave Serpent behind. This it did with pinpoint accuracy, the first blast reducing the tank to a shattered hulk, and the second obliterating the handful of Aspect Warriors who crawled from the burning wreckage.

At every turn, Imotekh sought to deny the Eldar their advantage of manoeuvrability. Deathmarks sniped jetbikers from their saddles. Flotillas of Heavy Destroyers positioned about the rim of the caldera targeted Falcons and Fire Prisms with volley after volley of crackling gauss fire, punching through hulls and disabling grav-units. By the time Starbane realised the severity of the threat he faced, his force was incapable of retreat and had no choice but to press on. Yet Imotekh's methodical countermeasures could only hold back the Eldar for only so long. For every crippled Necron that reassembled itself and rejoined the firing line, another succumbed to critical damage and was whisked away by retrieval teleporters. Little by little, the Stormlord's forces wore thin. The Monolith was destroyed in a bold assault by Fire Dragon Aspect Warriors, the Deathmarks eliminated by Pathfinders, and the Destroyers were scoured from their perch by Dark Reapers. And still the Eldar came – the main body of the host had arrived and were massing for a second attack. Imotekh knew that his remaining forces could not hold against this new wave of attackers – but then, it had never been the plan to do so. Summoning angry storm clouds to cover his retreat, Imotekh unsealed the great stone entrance and led his dwindling army in to the darkness of the tomb. Had Starbane been less arrogant, less certain of his superiority, he might have recognised the trap for what it was and withdrawn. Yet the Farseer cast his runes in haste and he saw only victory ahead, and so missed subtle warnings hidden amongst the skeins of fate.

Long did the Eldar walk in the darkness, through dusty vaults and chambers that had not been seen by the living for millions of years. Though they caught sight of many technological wonders, the intruders caught not so much as a glimpse of the Necrons they pursued, nor the tomb's robotic servitors. The deeper Starbane progressed into the tomb without any contact, the more he grew convinced that the enemy had simply fled, escaping into the labyrinth in order to fight another day. Deeper and deeper into the tomb the Eldar went until, in a colossal vaulted chamber many miles beneath the surface, Imotekh sprang his trap. Without warning, quantum force fields flickered into life at the chamber's exits, sealing the Eldar within.

THE TRAP IS SPRUNG

As his followers turned their weaponry on the force fields, Starbane could just make out the figure of Imotekh through the shimmering barrier, the impassive Phaeron standing mute and proud at the head of a phalanx of Immortals. Starbane saw the Stormlord raise one clenched fist in salute, then the buzzing began. It started as a low drone that rumbled through the stone floor, rising in volume and intensity until it drowned out any other sound. As the noise reached fever pitch, swirling clouds of blood-red nanoscarabs burst from concealed vents. They swarmed about the intruders, probing armour for any crack that would allow ingress, then burrowing into the warm flesh beneath. Then, as soon as it had begun, the buzzing ceased; the swarm of nanoscarabs dissipated. The flagstones of the chamber were slick with blood, and the air thick with the screams of the wounded, but Starbane was grimly jubilant – Imotekh's trap had been sprung, but the Eldar had endured it. The Farseer looked beyond the force field, a challenge in his eyes as he met Imotekh's gaze once again. In reply, the Stormlord tilted his head slightly to one side – though his expression was incapable of change, there was something distinctly mocking in his aspect. Then the Flayed Ones attacked.

The Flayed Ones dropped out of the darkness, their mad voices keening with bloodlust as their razor-sharp claws slashed and tore at the intruders. In the face of this new threat, the quantum shields were swiftly forgotten, the Eldar

gathering into knots of warriors who fought back to back against their attackers. It was impossible to say how long the gangrel creatures had lurked in the shadows, clutching to the vaulted ceiling. Perhaps they had been there before the Eldar had entered the chamber, perhaps they had been drawn by the bloodswarm scarabs – it mattered little. Initially, the Flayed Ones wrought great carnage, isolating individual Guardians and Aspect Warriors from their fellows and tearing them limb from limb. Yet, as the Eldar resistance grew less panicked and their defensive ring grew ever tighter, the tide began to turn. The Flayed Ones attacked again and again, only to be hurled back by the disciplined shuriken fire of Guardians and Aspect Warriors who fought shoulder-to-shoulder and back-to-back. The Flayed Ones attacked once, twice, three times more, then warily circled their prey, searching for an opening.

It was only when the Flayed Ones stalled their attack that Imotekh unleashed the final phase of his trap. With a gesture, the Stormlord negated the force field that stood before him, and ordered his minions into the fray. The Immortals advanced, firing indiscriminately as they came, uncaring as to whether their shots hit Eldar or Flayed One. For their part, the Flayed Ones were able to escape the threat, twisting aside and melting into the shadows as swiftly as they had come. For the Eldar, gathered in a tight formation to better defend against the Flayed Ones, the onslaught was devastating – nearly half their number fell to the first volley, and those that survived were so disoriented that their counterattack did little to stay the implacable Necron advance. By the time Imotekh led a shield wall of Lychguard into the chamber, the outcome of the battle was no longer in doubt.

Of the Eldar warriors who entered the tomb, only one survived to bring news of the defeat to Craftworld Alaitoc. In the Chamber of Eternal Starlight, Eldorath Starbane stood before the Seer Council and recounted the slaughter in the catacombs. The Farseer told of how Imotekh had spared him whilst all other captives had been swiftly put to death. He told how the Stormlord had severed his right hand to serve as a humiliating reminder of the defeat, and then set him loose. Starbane's words brought great dismay, and the council turned swiftly to plans of vengeance. Their next strike would not fall against Somonor, but at the very heart of the Sautekh Dynasty itself…

'Let me tell you of my future. My hand will reach out into the stars, reshaping the galaxy into a place of order and unity. Under my reign, the kingdoms of old shall live again, reborn to an age of power and glory the like of which you can only imagine. I will rule every planet touched by the light of this star and, even in the darkness beyond, my name will be whispered with fear and respect.

Your future, by contrast, is looking less than glorious – you will not be reaching out your hand to anything ever again, I think. Embrace the pain and humiliation of its loss, so that you might better learn the lessons from your defeat. Learn them well enough, and you might even be reborn as an enemy worthy of my attention. A hand is a measly price for such a gift, is it not?'

- Imotekh the Stormlord to Eldorath Starbane,
in the wake of the Siege of Somonor

A NEW EPOCH BEGINS

Humanity is widespread throughout the stars and encounters the Necrons with some frequency, but there is no mechanism by which the experiences of one embattled world can be shared with the wider Imperium. Even if there were, by what means would the data be catalogued? Hundreds of human worlds are depopulated or destroyed every year, and if their fates are noted at all, the cause of their demise is rarely discovered. There is no single repository of information in the Imperium, no established historical record – in a galaxy-spanning civilisation so shrouded in ignorance, it would be remarkable if it were otherwise.

Some Imperial scholars hold the slaughter at Sanctuary 101 in 897.M41 to be the first contact with Necrons. Such men do so in ignorance of the many millions of encounters that, though predating the Sanctuary 101 event, went entirely unremarked because no one survived to make note of them, the records were lost or deemed mythic, or simply took place on a world where the inhabitants made no distinction between differing alien perils. More so, it displays the classic arrogance of men who assume that the boundaries of their knowledge are, in fact, the boundaries of reality.

c744.M41 — The Return of the Silent King

The Silent King enters the bounds of the galaxy once more. Having encountered the Tyranids in the intergalactic void, he recognises the threat they pose to the Necrons' apotheosis – if the Tyranids devour all life in the galaxy, the Necrons will never find living bodies to house their consciousnesses. Thus does the Silent King break his self-imposed exile with the goal of marshalling his people against this new threat.

However, the Silent King has not anticipated the torpor in which the majority of the Necrons still lie. Many Tomb Worlds have been destroyed over the aeons, others still slumber and most of those that have awoken are still disoriented or somehow damaged. The Silent King is therefore forced to re-evaluate his plans. Working with the surviving Triarch Praetorians, he begins a pilgrimage across the galaxy, stirring those Tomb Worlds yet to revive, and speeding the recovery of those Tomb Worlds already awake. It is the Silent King's wish that the younger races' flawed attempts to destroy the Tyranids do not simply feed the Hive Fleets beyond the point where even a united Necron people have any hope of victory.

781.M41 — Storm Clouds Gather

After long years of preparation, Imotekh the Stormlord assumes control of the Crownworld of Mandragora and begins his conquest of the galaxy.

793.M41 — Raid on Solemnace

Following the onset of Hive Fleet Behemoth, the xenobiologists and Inquisitors of the Imperium are left with many questions that require answers. One such question brings Inquisitor Helynna Valeria to the ghost world Solemnace, seeking an explanation for why that world had gone untouched when all other planets in the Hive Fleet's path now lie destroyed.

Nothing could have prepared Valeria for what she finds in the silent darkness beneath Solemnace's pitted and barren surface: endless catacombs of advanced technology, long-lost artefacts from the Imperium's history and gallery after gallery of intricate life-size holographic sculptures laid out in silent tableau to commemorate historic scenes.

Valeria's party is briefly awestruck by what they discover, but then the entire Tomb World comes to angry life. Wave after wave of Canoptek Scarabs and Necron Warriors descend from all sides and the still air is filled with the whine of discharging gauss weapons. Seeking to regain the initiative for her beset followers, Valeria leads a charge against the shadowy figure orchestrating the carnage. Sighting carefully, Valeria unleashes a pulse from her graviton beamer that reduces the Necron Lord to mangled and fused scrap. Yet moments later, an identical figure emerges from the darkness, hale and undamaged. This time Valeria plunges the Dagger of Midnight's blade into her adversary's heart, yet even as her opponent's sparking frame sinks to the ground, another identical Necron Lord strides forwards, trampling the now-faceless ruin at her feet.

With that, Valeria orders a retreat back to the shuttles. Only a handful of the expeditionaries survive to reach their destination, and they do so empty-handed. Much to Valeria's disappointment, the Tomb World of Solemnace keeps all of its glorious secrets.

798.M41 — The Siege of Somonor

Imotekh the Stormlord repels an Alaitoc war host from the Tomb World of Somonor.

799.M41 — The End of Waaagh! 'Eadcrumpa

Big Mek 'Eadcrumpa leads his Waaagh! to the newly awakened Tomb World of Suranas. After initial skirmishes prove his still lethargic Necrons to be no match for the Orks, Lord Nepthk strikes a pact with 'Eadcrumpa. In exchange for several dozen functioning doomsday cannons, 'Eadcrumpa agrees to leave Suranas and seek plunder elsewhere (whilst secretly resolving to return to Suranas at a later date). Three months later, when the Waaagh! descends on the agri world of Eden Prime, 'Eadcrumpa is unable to resist his urge to investigate the doomsday cannons' systems. One breached containment core later and 'Eadcrumpa, his Waaagh! and the planet Eden Prime are erased from existence.

805.M41   The Ruin of Morrigar

A battle between hive gangs on Morrigar inadvertently awakens the Necron Tomb hidden there. All contact with Morrigar is lost shortly thereafter. When the Cadian 207th makes planetfall six months later, there is no trace of any inhabitants, human or otherwise. Before the Imperial Guard can leave Morrigar, the nomadic Necron warlord, Anrakyr the Traveller, arrives. Assuming the humans are responsible for the apparent destruction of the Tomb World, he launches an attack that leaves his own forces decimated and the Cadian 207th utterly eliminated.

813.M41   Escape from Cano'var

At Nemesor Zahndrekh's instruction, the armies of Gidrim invade the Tau world of Cano'var, routing the planetary defenders after two weeks of campaigning. The Necron victory is short-lived however. A demi-company of White Scars, led by Kor'sarro Khan, arrive on Cano'var, pursuing a now-obsolete punitive mission against the previous inhabitants. An overwhelming volley of gauss fire destroys the White Scars Thunderhawks moments after they land, leaving Khan and his Battle-Brothers to fight a bold, but doomed, series of hit-and-run battles. Almost all of the White Scars are slain on Uzme Plateau, but Zahndrekh commands that Kor'sarro Khan is spared and imprisoned.

So does Khan begin a peculiar period of captivity beneath the surface of Cano'var. Zahndrekh treats him with honour, though few of the other Necron Lords even acknowledge his presence. At a bizarre feast, where food is placed before Zahndrekh and his court but goes uneaten, Khan learns he is but one of a dozen prisoners. With the desire for freedom outweighing any ranklement or rivalry, Khan and the other captives conspire to escape.

The Necrons are slow to react and so the breakout goes well at first. Only when Vargard Obyron takes command do things go badly for the escapees. Several of the fugitives are slain by Obyron's warscythe, leaving only Kor'sarro and an Eldar Ranger by the name of Illic Nightspear to fight on, and the latter swiftly receives a blow that sends him sprawling from the fight. Thus does the battle devolve into a duel atop bleeding bodies and broken machines. Khan's sword is quicker and guided by a desperate fury, but Obyron's body repairs any damage within moments. Little by little, Khan tires, and the sweeping warscythe comes closer to connecting with each swing. Finally, one of the Vargard's blows is too swift for Khan to evade – the warscythe slices through his armour and deep into his flesh. Before Obyron can finish his foe, there is an intervention from an unexpected source.

Unknown to either combatant, Zahndrekh has been watching the fight from afar and, impressed by Khan's skill and bravery, orders Obyron to stand aside and let him leave. Dragging the crippled Nightspear behind, Khan finally escapes to the surface, finds a still functioning Tau craft and leaves Cano'var far behind.

Khan and Nightspear part ways shortly after, the Eldar to his craftworld and the White Scar to Chogoris. Shortly after Khan's return to his Chapter Planet, Nemesor Zahndrekh and Vargard Obyron are added to Scrolls of Vengeance, their names to be put forward as possible quarry for the next Great Hunt.

815.M41   The Disappearance of Explorator Fleet 913

Explorator Fleet 913 strays into territory controlled by the Tomb World of Gheden and is destroyed by the fleet of Nemesor Azderon. When the battle is done, wreckage is set adrift in the projected trajectory of Alaitoc Craftworld. By the time three Companies of Ultramarines come in search of the Explorator Fleet, Azderon has long withdrawn, but the presence of Alaitoc's pathfinder vessels draw the Space Marines into conflict with the Eldar.

824.M41   The Return of Thaszar the Invincible

The shadow-shrouded world of Athonos is wracked by severe earth tremors. The cause remains a mystery until a colossal Tomb Ship captained by the pirate king, Thaszar the Invincible, emerges from beneath the ground, shedding soil, rock and fragments of hab-block from its hull as it rises. The world's defences are, understandably, in disarray. Fortunately for the inhabitants, Thaszar has yet to realise that humans are an intelligent form of life, and pays no more attention to the panicked defenders than he would to a nest of insects. The Athonosian planetary capital lies in ruins, but the rest of the planet survives relatively unscathed as the Tomb Ship heads into the stars, towards the Tomb World of Zapennec, pausing only to obliterate a holo-stealthed Eldar listening post hidden in near orbit.

829.M41   The Enslavement of Aryand

Overlord Vitokh masterminds the invasion of hive world Aryand. After a long and bloody siege, Aryand's governor accepts Vitokh's terms and Aryand becomes a slave world in service to the Necron dynasty of Altymhor.

831.M41   The Dissolution of Burr

After a long archaeological expedition on the mysterious planet of Phall, famed explorer Benedict Draconis returns to the binary worlds of Burr. The planetary governor holds a banquet in Draconis' honour, which proves to be a fatal mistake when a swarm of mindshackle scarabs burst bloodily from the explorator's brain to feast on the governor and his guests. From there, the mindshackle scarabs multiply and swiftly infest Burr's military echelons.

With his trap sprung and much of the binary worlds' defences thus under his control, Overlord Janzikh of Phall launches an invasion. Burr Major is the first planet to fall, thanks to recklessness on the part of its remaining defenders, but soon both worlds are firmly under Necron control. The dissolution furnaces roar day and night, and when Captain D'Estev and the Fire Lords' 5th Company finally arrive, all they can do is destroy Janzikh in retaliation for his deeds.

857.M41   The Lazar Blockade

Seeking vengeance for the destruction wrought upon their 4th Company, the Silver Skulls blockade the Lazar system and attempt to purge the Necrons from the its planets. Though the main Tomb World is overwhelmed and obliterated, the Silver Skulls are quick to regret their hasty assault, as secondary bases throughout the system whir into life. Unable to admit defeat, the Silver Skulls dig in, and what should have been a simple exercise in reciprocity becomes a gruelling campaign.

859.M41   The Traveller Has Come

Anrakyr the Traveller arrives in the embattled Lazar system, and immediately joins his forces to those defending against the Silver Skulls' onslaught. Necron victory is finally assured at the Battle of Dreadpeak, when Anrakyr's Pyrrhian Eternals spearhead an assault on the Silver Skulls' downed battle barge *Argent Hammer*.

Though the Space Marines battle hard against the veterans of Pyrrhia, their efforts are undone when Anrakyr seizes control over the battle barge's still-functioning weapon batteries and turns their fury on the defenders. With their Chapter Master slain and their forces in disarray, the Silver Skulls are forced to withdraw their blockade of Lazar – though they take great care to ensure that word of their defeat does not spread. His duty done, Anrakyr takes ship and heads out into the galaxy once more.

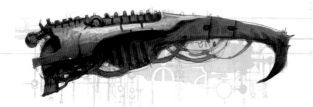

897.M41   Massacre at Sanctuary 101

The armies of the Sautekh Dynasty continue their relentless advance across the Vidar sector. Imotekh the Stormlord leads an attack on the fortress convent on Sanctuary 101. The Sisters of Battle within are slaughtered to the last.

910.M41   The Storm Grows

Imotekh's campaigns are halted briefly by the Imperium's resolute defence of forge world Hypnoth. Imperial Guard and Space Marine reinforcements flood into the battle zone, and though they cannot achieve a lasting victory, they succeed in tying down the Necron assault for several months. Encouraged by the prophecies of the astromancer Orikan the Diviner, Imotekh finally breaks the stalemate by launching a series of attacks on Hypnoth's supply worlds, Praedis-Zeta and Nyx.

The first two raids perform entirely as expected, with the worlds laid waste and their vital supplies destroyed or claimed by the Sautekh forces. However, an unforeseen Tyranid infestation on Nyx wreaks havoc amongst the Necron forces and threatens to completely derail Imotekh's entire campaign. Nevertheless, Imotekh rises to the challenge, weaving a strategy that manipulates the Tyranid swarm into venting its fury on the remaining Imperial defenders. With both sides thus distracted, Imotekh is able to extricate his remaining forces.

911.M41   The Fall of Hypnoth

Sautekh Crypteks succeed in introducing a mechanophage into the defence systems of forge world Hypnoth, reducing its formidably-armed bastions to helpless ferrocrete shells. Despite a valorous defence by Flesh Tearers and Iron Hands Space Marines, Hypnoth is conquered within days.

912-926.M41   The Worldengine

A violent coup on the Tomb World of Borsis sees its introspective Lord replaced by one of a more expansionist bent. Thus are the long dormant engines of Borsis fired into life once more, signalling the start of a campaign that leaves much of the Vidar sector in ruins.

930.M41   Slaughter on Schrödinger VII

The forces of the Stormlord descend upon the frozen plains of Schrödinger VII. They drive the local defenders to the shelter of the labyrinthine cryonite mines, but are unable to prevent the planet's Astropath choir from dispatching a distress hymnal. A counterattack swiftly arrives in the form of a Black Templars strike force under the command of Marshal Helbrecht. Yet Imotekh is not caught by surprise so easily, and has already shifted his armies into a formidable defensive configuration.

Helbrecht's assault, intended as a crippling alpha strike, is instead blunted by a series of impeccably planned ambushes on the Drop Pod and Thunderhawk drop zones. As the frozen caverns echo to the roar of explosions, scores of Black Templars and Necrons alike are hurled into rivers of molten cryonite. Imotekh and Helbrecht meet in battle atop the stalactite-heavy span of an ice bridge. In the contest that follows, Helbrecht deals Imotekh a dozen ruinous blows, but each time the Phaeron recovers in a matter of seconds to land a strike of his own.

Helbrecht finally collapses, blood flowing from a score of serious wounds. However, instead of finishing his opponent, Imotekh brings his scythe down to sever Helbrecht's right hand to 'serve the Marshal as a much-deserved reminder of defeat'. Helbrecht is still roaring in fury and pain as Imotekh pitches him off the bridge to the cavern floor far below. The surviving Black Templars rally to their fallen Marshal's side and make a fighting retreat, leaving Schrödinger VII in the Stormlord's hands.

955.M41   Alliance at Devil's Crag
The Silent King reluctantly joins forces with the Blood Angels to defeat a Tyranid splinter fleet.

970.M41   The Hall of Swords
The Emperor's Swords Chapter of Space Marines, the second to bear that name, is destroyed when a Tomb World awakens beneath their fortress monastery on the world of Bellicas. Those forces isolated outside are swiftly overwhelmed, but the fate of those within is far grimmer. Subverting the systems of the fortress monastery, a conclave of Crypteks shut down the defences and entomb the Space Marines within their own citadel. Seeking sport from their captives, the new rulers of Bellicas take it in turns to lead waves of Necron Warriors through the shadowed halls, each with the aim of accruing more kills than this peers. Though the Space Marines fight with determination and never once surrender to terror, after three weeks the contest goes to Lord Trakesz for his personal decapitation of Captain Arnoc Voreign.

973.M41   The Rise of Damnos
By some fateful quirk, the Necron tomb on Damnos wakes swiftly to full function, overwhelming the human settlers and repelling a counterattack by the Ultramarines 2nd Company. The Necrons of Damnos then proceed to awaken their Dolmen Gates and reconquer a crucial spar of the webway, driving out the Eldar who had reclaimed its paths during the Great Sleep. With their webway access restored, raiding parties from Damnos reach out across the Ultima Segmentum, leaving carnage in their wake.

985.M41   Conqueror's Fall
The Stormlord's Tomb Ship *Inevitable Conqueror* comes under attack by a Black Templars fleet whilst en route to the Sautekh coreworld of Davatas. The architect of the assault is none other than Marshal Helbrecht, come searching for a long anticipated revenge upon the warlord who humbled him on Schrödinger VII. A broadside from the battle barge *Sigismund* strips away the *Conqueror's* shields an instant before the Black Templars' boarding torpedoes strike home and, within moments, the decks of the *Inevitable Conqueror* are swarming with vengeful Space Marines. Pride compels Imotekh to stand and fight, but his forces are in disarray and so logic wins out, dictating withdrawal. The Stormlord therefore teleports

to an escort vessel and makes his escape. Helbrecht is incandescent with fury at this foe's retreat, but consoles himself by personally setting Imotekh's beloved flagship on a collision course with a nearby star, and blasting to smithereens those other Necron craft too slow to flee.

999.M41   The Carnac Campaign
Anrakyr the Traveller arrives on a planet he supposes to be the Tomb World of Carnac, only to find it infested with Eldar Exodites. Realising the that tomb, if it remains, will be buried too deep for him to awaken it before the Exodites can themselves summon aid, Anrakyr entreats the Lords and Overlords of other Tomb Worlds for aid. Reinforcements swiftly arrive from Mandragora, Gidrim and Trakonn, though the most unexpected of all is a contingent from Solemnace, led by Trazyn the Infinite himself. All this takes time, however, and by the time the Night Scythe fleets deploy the invading forces, the armies of Alaitoc Craftworld stand side by side with the Exodites.

Guided by the prophecies of Farseer Eldorath Starbane and the strategies of Illic Nightspear, the Eldar attempt to stall the Necron invasion with a series of hit-and-run attacks. Their aim is to sever the command structure by destroying Anrakyr and his closest allies, but the Pyrrhian Lord manages to subvert the prophesies of the Farseer though the astromantic analyses of Orikan the Diviner. Though Orikan's divinations are by no means as focussed as those of Starbane, they are sufficient to tangle the skeins of fate and leave many details beyond the Farseer's reach. So it is that Pathfinders arrive at what they thought to be Anrakyr's location, only to find him long gone and squads of Deathmarks waiting in ambush.

After several inconclusive battles on Carnac's verdant plains, Anrakyr forces the Eldar to engage in a head-to-head confrontation by marching on the World Spirit shrine. As the tireless Necron legions advance upon the walls, Doom Scythes duel with Eldar fighters in the skies above, Deathmarks ply a deadly trade of ambush and counter-ambush with Alaitoc Pathfinders, and all the while Flayed Ones prowl the flanks, pouncing on any Eldar foolish enough to show even a momentary sign of weakness. The two sides are well matched, with Necron hardiness countered by the precise strikes of the Eldar. Victory finally falls to the Necrons when Carnac's tomb unexpectedly begins to awaken, stirred from dormancy by the tumult above. With Necron reinforcements now starting to trickle into the campaign, the Eldar have little choice but to abandon Carnac and its World Spirit to their foes.

Anrakyr is grimly jubilant in the campaign's aftermath, and gladly accedes when Trazyn requests the entire World Spirit shrine as spoils of war. For his part, Orikan requests no trophy or payment for victory, and merely hopes that when the flush of victory fades, no one thinks to question to the convenient coincidence of Carnac's awakening.

THE ARMY OF AEONS PAST

This section of the book details the forces used by the Necrons – their weapons, their units, and some famous special characters that you can choose, such as Trazyn the Infinite. Each entry describes a unit and gives the specific rules you needed to use it in your games. As such, the army list refers to the page numbers of these entries, so you can easily check back. This section is divided into two parts; the first describes all of the troops and vehicles fielded by the Necrons, including the special characters, while the second part details their armoury of weapons and equipment.

The army list shows all the standard and optional wargear available to each model. Some items of equipment are unique to a character or unit, while others are used by more than one unit. A unique item will be detailed in its owner's entry, while an item that is not unique, will be detailed in the wargear section. A good example is the Staff of the Destroyer, a weapon wielded by Imotekh the Stormlord. As such, its rules are detailed in Imotekh's entry. Imotekh also carries a gauntlet of fire. This weapon is also carried by other Necrons, and so its rules are found in the wargear section.

NECRON SPECIAL RULES

REANIMATION PROTOCOLS
Necrons have sophisticated self-repair systems that return even critically damaged warriors to the fight.

If a model with the Reanimation Protocols rule is removed as a casualty, there is a chance that it will self-repair and return to play at the end of the current phase. Whenever a unit takes one or more casualties, place counters or other suitable markers next to the unit to remind you how many casualties were taken. If the unit makes a fall back move, remove any counters from it – any damaged Necrons are left behind and self-destruct rather than risk capture by the enemy.

At the end of the phase, after any Morale checks have been taken and fall back moves have been made, roll a D6 for each Reanimation Protocols counter next to the unit. On a 1, 2, 3 or 4 the damage is too severe and no self-repair occurs – nothing happens. On a 5 or 6, a Necron reassembles itself and continues to fight – return one of the slain models to play with a single Wound, placed in coherency with a model from its unit that has not itself returned through Reanimation Protocols this phase. Models returning to play in this fashion must be placed at least 1" from enemy models. If the model's unit is engaged in close combat, the model immediately piles in. Models that cannot be placed in this way do not return.

Reanimation Protocols rolls cannot be attempted if the unit has been destroyed – once the last model has been removed as a casualty, remove all your counters. Note that characters do not count as part of the unit for the purposes of Reanimation Protocols – if a character is the only survivor of a unit, his presence is not sufficient to allow a Reanimation Protocols roll, so remove any remaining counters. Once all Reanimation Protocols rolls have been made for a unit (passed or failed) remove all your counters from the unit.

EVER-LIVING
If a model with this special rule is removed as a casualty, do not add a Reanimation Protocols counter to its unit. Instead place an Ever-living counter where the model was removed from play. At the end of the phase, roll for this counter, just as you would for a Reanimation Protocols counter.

If the model had joined a unit when it was removed as a casualty, and the roll was passed, it must be returned to play, with a single Wound, in coherency with that unit as explained in Reanimation Protocols. If the model had not joined a unit when it was removed as a casualty, it must be returned to play, with a single Wound, within 3" of the the counter. In either case, the model must be placed at least 1" away from enemy models. If the model is placed in coherency with one or more friendly units that it is eligible to join, it automatically joins one of those units (your choice). If the model was locked in close combat when it 'died', and the combat is ongoing, then it must immediately pile in. If the returning model cannot be placed, for whatever reason, it is lost and does not return. If the roll was failed, remove the counter from play.

ENTROPIC STRIKE
Necron technology can break down even hardened armour plate into wisps of energy.

Any model that suffers one or more unsaved Wounds from a weapon or model with this special rule immediately loses its armour save for the remainder of the battle (effectively altering its armour save to '-'). For each hit a vehicle suffers from a weapon or model with this special rule, roll a D6. For each result of 4+, it immediately loses 1 point of Armour Value from all facings. If a vehicle is reduced to Armour 0 on any facing, it is immediately wrecked.

LIVING METAL
Necron vehicles are composed of a semi-sentient alloy capable of incredible feats of resilience and self-repair.

If a model with this special rule suffers a 'crew shaken' result, roll a D6: on a roll of 1, the result is applied normally; on a roll of 2+, the result is ignored. If a model with this special rule suffers a 'crew stunned' result, roll a D6: on a roll of 1-3 the result is applied normally; on a roll of 4+, the result is ignored.

NECRON LORDS & OVERLORDS

As befitted their rank, the nobles of the Necron kingdoms emerged far better from biotransference than did the plebeian classes. Not only were their new bodies stronger and more durable, but the engrammic circuitry that housed each noble's intellect and personality was far more extensive than that granted to lesser Necrontyr. Most Necrons emerge from the Great Sleep as dull-witted creatures, with little memory of the individual they once were. By contrast, unless they suffer damage during their dormancy, Necron Lords and Overlords retain all the drives, obsessions and nuances of personality that they once possessed.

A Tomb World may have dozens, or even hundreds, of nobles, but only one has the power of absolute rule. For coreworlds and fringeworlds this is usually a Lord, while crownworlds and particularly important coreworlds will have Overlords as their regents. Each Phaeron will also lay claim to a crownworld, from which he rules his entire dynasty.

Amongst a Tomb World's nobles, political infighting is rife and there are always insidious schemes playing out, albeit at an interminable pace. As a result of their android nature, Necrons tend towards calculative behaviour, and a pretender will rarely move openly if the chances of success are outweighed by the probability of failure. Similarly, it is not unknown for a challenged Overlord to yield to a subordinate if there is no hope of immediate victory, choosing to wait out the years and centuries in a lower rank, patiently anticipating an opportunity to reclaim that which was lost.

Yet if the prize is large enough, power struggles can erupt into open conflict. When this occurs, the remainder of the Tomb World's nobles align according to loyalty and ambition, though some will wait as long as possible before doing so whilst they negotiate the price of their loyalty. These internal wars invariably follow the formalised codes that governed the ancient Necrontyr, leading to set piece battles with forces arranged and rules agreed in advance by the competitors. In times before biotransference, such events led to the slaughter of countless millions in a matter of days or weeks. Nowadays, thanks to the Necrons' capacity for self-repair, these wars can last for years or even centuries with no discernible victor – reason enough for all but the most desperate or power-hungry Necron nobles to avoid such an outcome.

For every battle a Necron noble fights amongst his own kind, he will orchestrate hundreds of sprawling campaigns against alien usurpers who squat amongst the remains of the Necron dynasties. For many nemesors, it is unthinkable to honour an alien enemy with the traditional codes of battle. In their eyes, most races are little more than vermin to be wiped away with as much efficiency and as little pomp as possible. Most of the more advanced races, such as the Eldar, have simply proven themselves unworthy of being treated as equals. So it is that assassination and ambush – forms of battle forbidden in wars between the nobility – are employed against outsiders without reservation. Yet no matter how base a Necron ruler might consider his enemy to be, he personally oversees his battles wherever possible, leading his vassals from the thick of the fighting. Thus does he prove his superiority, both to his immediate peers and to adversaries in the galaxy at large.

When a Necron Lord or Overlord strides forth in his raiment of war, only the strongest and canniest of enemies have any hope of survival. His armoured form is proof against tank-busting weaponry; his metal sinews have might enough to crush bones to powder. At his command are all the arcane armaments of his ancient civilisation: warscythes, tachyon arrows and other wondrous tools of destruction. Yet perhaps a Necron noble's most potent weapon is his mind. Indeed, a Phaeron has so much force of will that he can infuse nearby minions with a portion of his own burning determination, creating an unstoppable core of resistance to any foe.

	WS	BS	S	T	W	I	A	Ld	Sv
Necron Overlord	4	4	5	5	3	2	3	10	3+
Necron Lord	4	4	5	5	1	2	2	10	3+

UNIT TYPE: Infantry (Character).

WARGEAR: Staff of light.

SPECIAL RULES: Ever-living, Independent Character (Necron Overlord only), Reanimation Protocols.

UPGRADES:

Phaeron: A Phaeron, and any unit he is with, have the Relentless special rule.

DESTROYER LORDS

Not all Necrons awaken from the great sleep as hale as was intended. Some suffer physical damage in the intervening millennia; usually faulty stasis-crypts bring on a slow decay that rots the mechanical body and erodes engrammic pathways. Others become infected by the flayer virus and devolve into creatures whose reason is subsumed by a taste for flesh. Yet there are also those Necrons who awaken from slumber with their physical form intact but their psyche torn beyond recovery. Angered and despairing of their soulless existence, these Necrons turn to nihilism. They no longer seek redemption or repatriation with the flesh that was so long lost to them. They wish only to drive all other living things into death's welcoming embrace. These then, are the Destroyers, the self-appointed heralds of oblivion.

Destroyer Lords are the most maniacal of their kind. This is chiefly because they retain far more intellect than baseline Destroyers, and can bring all of this fearsome intelligence to bear in their pursuit of galactic conquests. This efficiency is all the more murderous for the Destroyer Lord's complete lack of empathy. Whilst few Necrons retains any instinctive comprehension of pity and mercy, the cleverest amongst them can at least still grasp such concepts intellectually. Not so Destroyer Lords – they have long ago discarded any ability to empathise with other creatures. If a Destroyer Lord takes prisoners, it is not out of honour or pity, but simple efficiency. There are a thousand ways in which captives can be used as lures for other fleshlings, and Destroyer Lords are conversant with every last one. Indeed, in a galaxy full to overspilling with genocidal despots, Destroyer Lords remain worthy of mention as something truly horrific. Where others kill for pleasure, or in service to some malignant god, Destroyer Lords pursue their bloody crusade simply because it is their chosen course. By their calculation, joy is just one more pointless emotion, and the favour of gods naught but a crutch to support the frailties of flesh.

In truth, even Overlords find Destroyer Lords somewhat disconcerting, believing them to have too willingly embraced the machine. Most also hold the lingering suspicion that when all organic life in the galaxy has been eliminated, their nihilistic brethren will turn on their own kind. As a result, many Destroyer Lords are outcasts and pariahs. Stripped of title and rank, they are forced to dwell on the periphery of Necron civilisation, lest their madness prove infectious.

Destroyer Lords are formidable combatants, for their physical might equals that of the mightiest Overlords. Most favour warscythes or voidblades over ranged tools of war. In his horrific way, a Destroyer Lord is a craftsman, and the fruits of his bloody labours are far more easily tallied in the thick of the fighting. There is no artistry to a Destroyer Lord's blows – each swing of his blade is driven by the desire for optimum efficiency. Strangely, this often means a Destroyer Lord's attacks are unintentionally spectacular. If he calculates that three enemies can be slain swifter with one blow than three individual strikes, then a single blow is all that will be made. A lesser creature would perhaps balk at such a risk, but for a Destroyer Lord, who has calculated success down the tiniest detail, there is no risk to be had – only deadly certainty.

	WS	BS	S	T	W	I	A	Ld	Sv
Destroyer Lord	4	4	5	6	3	2	3	10	3+

UNIT TYPE: Jump Infantry (Character).

WARGEAR: Warscythe.

SPECIAL RULES: Ever-living, Independent Character, Preferred Enemy (Everything!), Reanimation Protocols.

'I acknowledge no master, save for the almighty spectre of death. In its name, I will reap all signs of life from this galaxy, leaving nothing but a barren monument to timeless inevitability.

Call it what you will, but this is the pursuit of nothing less than absolute perfection. Those who cannot understand its necessity are clearly flawed, but they should not despair – I will ensure that they do not live to see the final stage of the work completed.'

- Executioner Ezandrakh of the Mephrit Dynasty
Herald of the Red Harvest

CRYPTEKS

Crypteks are members of pan-galactic conclaves of technologists whose purpose is to study and maintain the eldritch devices of their race. They are masters of dimensional dissonance, singularity manipulation, atomic transmutation, elemental transmogrification and countless other reason-defying technologies. In many ways, a Cryptek's powers mirror those employed by the psykers of other races, but with a crucial difference; instead of using a mutant mind to channel Warp energies, the Cryptek employs arcane science to harness the universe's fundamental forces.

Every conclave specialises in a particular field of techno-sorcery, be it psychomancy, plasmancy, chronomancy or any one of a hundred thousand other disciplines. The conclaves were originally founded to share information and expertise from one end of the galaxy to the other, but have since become fragmented and isolated. In the millennia since biotransference, Crypteks have become just as stagnant and fragmented as every other aspect of Necron society. Nowadays, the surviving conclaves are maintained out of force of habit more than for any practical reason.

Though Crypteks have no official rank in the political structure of a dynasty, they wield incredible influence. Necrontyr nobility were ever disinterested by the workings of the technology they employed, and this attitude has faded little with time. A Cryptek's power springs from this ignorance, and from the army of Canoptek Spyders, Wraiths and Scarabs under his control. Though few Necron nobles pay the idea much heed, a Tomb World's countless systems require perpetual maintenance if they are to function at peak efficiency, and a slighted Cryptek is always willing to bring the maintenance cycle to a screaming halt should his 'betters' require a reminder. Even the proudest Overlord will muster an apology when his soldiers and weapons seize up.

On occasion, a Necron Overlord will go so far as to recruit a particularly trusted and knowledgeable Cryptek to serve in his Royal Court. Such a move can prove politically dangerous for the Overlord, as this essentially elevates the Cryptek to the same rank as the Necron Lords already serving there, and so inevitably fosters resentment amongst his regal subordinates. Nonetheless, having the Cryptek's wealth of knowledge and expertise close at hand is normally viewed as more than adequate compensation for the risk.

Ultimately, the only thing that holds the ambitions of a Cryptek in check is another of his kind. Should a retained Cryptek rise too far above his station, a Necron Overlord will attempt to replace him by luring a different, and more tractable, Cryptek away from the service of a rival. Even this has complications, for whilst no Cryptek will knowingly supplant another of the same conclave, a rival from another conclave will happily do so. Inevitably, such plots and counterplots can lead to rivalry, or even outright conflict, between different Crypteks and conclaves. This, in turn, can lead to duels of techno-sorcery that inevitably result in the losing Cryptek suffering a most unpleasant, if scientifically impressive, fate – such as being transmuted into liquid adamantium, moved a nanosecond out of phase with the rest

of the universe or being transformed into a speck of dwarf-star matter and hurled across the galaxy.

Once his services are acquired, a Cryptek's duties stretch far beyond the Tomb World. Indeed, it is common procedure for an Overlord to grant a Cryptek the first pickings of precious alloys, power cores and focus crystals in exchange for his services on campaign. Such a bargain serves both sides well; resources on a Tomb World are limited, and the Cryptek's trade requires that he have a ready supply of raw materials. For his part, the Overlord gains the full fury of the Cryptek's incredible techno-sorceries. With a mere gesture of his staff, a Cryptek can bring the ground to writhing and hungry life beneath the enemy's feet, set the very air ablaze, summon clouds of soul-sapping darkness or call down eldritch bolts of living lightning. These are the weapons of the gods, and only gods would think to stand against them.

	WS	BS	S	T	W	I	A	Ld	Sv
Cryptek	4	4	4	4	1	2	1	10	4+

UNIT TYPE: Infantry (Character).

WARGEAR: Staff of light.

SPECIAL RULES: Ever-living, Reanimation Protocols.

NECRON WARRIORS

Necron Warriors form the cold heart of a Tomb World's armies. They are implacable, emotionless and terrifying soldiers – the inexorable emissaries of death itself. Yet on closer inspection of a Necron Warrior, aberrant details become visible that act against the image of the inevitable reaper. Its reactions, though precise, are slow. Its limbs, though strong and sleek, are pitted and corroded, covered with an oily fluid seeping from aged joints. Its movements are jerky, and every so often it stumbles as synapses misfire. In truth, the Necron Warrior would almost be pitiable were it not for the merciless gleam flickering in its eyes and the pervasive sense that it is less a sentient creature than it is one of the walking dead.

Unlike other forces at a nemesor's command, Necron Warriors are in no way autonomous. They are bound entirely to their commander's unyielding will. Outside of simple instructions, a Necron Warrior's tactical awareness is almost entirely nonexistent. Without more specific orders, a phalanx of Necron Warriors automatically settles into a guard routine, repelling enemy attacks with rippling volleys of precision gauss fire. All this they do in utter silence, for Necron Warriors never speak – vocalisation was a luxury deliberately denied them by design. However, if heavily damaged, a Necron Warrior emits a modulated electronic scream, a tooth-rattling shriek that is an eerie parody of a living creature's pain. It is impossible to say whether this death wail is intended as a warning to other Necrons, or is simply a half-remembered reaction to the onset of oblivion.

What Necron Warriors lack in intuition they more than make up for in determination and durability. Once orders have been received, they are completely single-minded and will follow commands through to conclusion without question. Furthermore, individual warriors can suffer grievous damage before they cease fighting. Even dismemberment or decapitation cannot be counted upon to stay a Necron Warrior's advance, for its sophisticated self-repair mechanisms can return it to the fray within minutes.

Despite its tenuous sensory connection to reality, a Necron Warrior is not entirely fearless. Though most of its animalistic instincts have long since been expunged or degraded into nothingness, a Necron Warrior's need for self-preservation still has some purchase on its mind. That said, such a reaction requires it to have registered the danger at hand, something which is by no means certain. Should survival instinct go untriggered, the Necron Warrior will carry its fight to almost unbelievable degrees, marching heedlessly through minefields, bombardments or other battlefield hazards that will surely see it destroyed.

It is possible that the Necron Warriors' paucity of wit and self-identity are merely side-effects of the biotransference process. In the Time of Flesh they were not soldiers, but artisans, merchants, farmers, scribes – indeed anything but creatures of war. As citizens of lesser status it was inevitable that their conversion would be neither so careful nor so precise as that of the Necron soldiery or royalty. Even more disturbing is the idea that the Necron Warriors' dull-wittedness might well have been a deliberate part of the design; that those Necron nobles who oversaw biotransference deliberately stripped their vassals of personality, character and awareness to ensure that they would have loyal and unswerving foot soldiers in the endless battles to come.

	WS	BS	S	T	W	I	A	Ld	Sv
Necron Warrior	4	4	4	4	1	2	1	10	4+

UNIT TYPE: Infantry.

WARGEAR: Gauss flayer.

SPECIAL RULES: Reanimation Protocols.

'Wit is not required in my vassals; they need only the ability to fight and die in the furtherance of my boundless glory. Only the most merciful and beneficent of rulers would spare their subjects from the burden of independence, do you not agree?'

- Thaszar the Invincible
Phaeron of the Sarnekh Dynasty
Supreme Warbringer of the Crownworld of Zapennec

The Army of Aeons Past

NECRON IMMORTALS

When the Necrons first conquered the galaxy, they did so through the unfaltering and implacable onslaught of legion upon legion of Immortals. These were the very elite of the Necrontyr armies, hardened veterans born anew in tireless metal bodies. For hundreds of years, the Immortals were a scourge upon all who stood between the Necrons and galactic domination. Now, the Immortal legions are but an echo of what they once were, for countless trillions were destroyed in the final days of the War in Heaven. Yet billions more survived, and now wait only to be awakened from their tombs and begin the reconquest of the galaxy.

As the shock troops of a Tomb World's armies, Immortals have a far wider range and depth of reaction than Necron Warriors, for they have retained much of their tactical and strategic experience. Indeed, in many ways the transfer to machine bodies and minds only sharpened the Immortals' ability to prosecute war in an efficient fashion. Left to their own devices, a phalanx of Immortals continues to strive for victory using every tactic and stratagem at their disposal. This is not to say that Immortals do not have shortcomings. Most profound is the fact that they are incapable of learning and adapting to new means of battle. On the rare occasions when Immortals are presented with a battlefield situation that cannot be conquered by ancient tactics, they will apply the counterstrategy they consider the closest match, regardless of its ultimate suitability. Fortunately, such instances are unusual for, no matter the advances in technology, war has changed little since the days of the War in Heaven.

Immortals are capable of speech, albeit in flat and emotionless tones that are even more soulless than the hollow voices of the Overlords. This enables them to not only provide clinically precise battlefield reports to their superiors, but also to issue orders to Necron Warriors, a factor that often increases the efficiency of the entire battlefront. Outside these parameters, Immortals are, at best, limited conversationalists, often falling prey to recursive loops of logic and procedure in place of conveying any pertinent information. If presented with an enquiry or concept beyond its understanding, an Immortal simply does not respond. This trait only serves to encourage the more arrogant Necron Overlords in their rambling and rhetorical soliloquies. This, in turn, ensures that a nemesor's pre-battle address to his troops can drag on for an interminably long time, as he scours his Immortals' silent forms for some glimmer of understanding and they, with patience born of utter incomprehension, stare straight back at him, waiting solemnly for the order that will throw them into battle once more.

What Immortals lack in flexibility of approach, they more than make up for in durability and firepower. Immortals are more thickly armoured than Necron Warriors and can weather a storm of heavy bolter or assault cannon fire with little more to show for it than fresh carbon-scoring on their already time-worn frames. Even should an Immortal be felled, its threat is not ended, for its auto-repair systems are, if anything, the tiniest fraction more efficient than that of the baseline warriors. Few foes can withstand the Immortals' return fire so easily. A single shot from a gauss blaster can punch through most types of armour to strip flesh from bone, and the closer the Immortals come to their target, the shorter the interval between blistering volleys. At that point, all the foe can do is dive for cover, but this offers only a fool's hope of survival. There can be no hiding from Immortals – their gauss blasters will scour every nook and cranny until naught remains but ash on the breeze.

	WS	BS	S	T	W	I	A	Ld	Sv
Necron Immortal	4	4	4	4	1	2	1	10	3+

UNIT TYPE: Infantry.

WARGEAR: Gauss blaster.

SPECIAL RULES: Reanimation Protocols.

'With a dozen legions of Immortals at my command, I could humble the stars themselves. One will be more than sufficient to crush your pathetic world.'

- *Imotekh the Stormlord*
Phaeron of the Sautekh Dynasty
Regent of Mandragora

LYCHGUARDS

In ancient times, Lychguards were the wardens of the nobility, said to be incorruptible and utterly dedicated to their charges. Then, such an assertion was as much propaganda as it was truth. Though the Lychguards doubtless possessed greater loyalty than the common run of soldiery, they were still but mortal and prone to all the temptations and weaknesses to which flesh is heir. Now, Lychguards are indeed that which legend made them. They are no longer capable of straying from their master's edicts – careful engram manipulation during biotransference saw to that. Each is programmed with unswerving loyalty to a particular noble, or sometimes to a whole dynasty. This, combined with the fact that they have retained most of their personality intact, makes Lychguards the ideal emissaries and lieutenants in situations deemed too dangerous to risk the existence of a Phaeron or his regal subordinates.

Physically, Lychguards are incredibly imposing, housed in the same heavily-armoured forms more commonly reserved for Necron royalty. This is mostly due to practicality – after all, what use is a bodyguard if he has not might and hardiness enough to defend his master? However, there is also an underlying arrogance to the Lychguards' thickly-armoured design, a brazenness meant to present an irresistible challenge to the noble's enemies. Accordingly, Lychguards can inevitably be found at the heart of any battle, either because their master's army has rallied around them, or the enemy has chosen to make the destruction of their charge, and therefore the destruction of the Lychguard, a priority.

As with much of the Necron army, a Lychguard's armament is decreed largely by tradition. Most are equipped with heavy-bladed warscythes drawn from their patron's personal armoury – when combined with a Lychguard's prodigious strength, there is very little such a blade cannot penetrate. Phalanxes employed by more influential Overlords instead carry hyperphase swords and dispersion shields, trading a little in the way of raw might in favour of the incredible protection granted by the dispersion shields' interlocking force barriers. Whilst such a squad might make slower progress as they carve their way through a Space Marine strike force, the ability to withstand anything from a siege shell to a defence laser blast is ample compensation.

Regardless of armament, a Lychguard always favours a single, dismembering strike over a flurry of lesser blows and will trust its own hardiness to hold the enemy at bay. Unlike lesser Necrons, Lychguards take pride in – and even relish – their bloody work. Indeed, for a Lychguard, anything less than a perfect strike is something to be regretted. Some Lychguard even go so far as to seek forgiveness from their sovereign if they land anything less than an immaculate stroke. So will a Lychguard sometimes stand motionless in the heat of battle,

its blade raised and unmoving whilst it awaits the most auspicious moment to strike. When that moment arrives, the Lychguard brings its blade about in an unstoppable arc to sever limbs, lop heads or cleave torsos in twain.

	WS	BS	S	T	W	I	A	Ld	Sv
Lychguard	4	4	5	5	1	2	2	10	3+

UNIT TYPE: Infantry.

WARGEAR: Warscythe.

SPECIAL RULES: Reanimation Protocols.

UPGRADES:
Dispersion shield: The force barrier projected by a dispersion shield can be used to fend off close combat attacks or deflect incoming enemy fire.

A Lychguard with a dispersion shield has a 4+ invulnerable save. If this save is made against a shooting attack, choose an unengaged enemy unit within 6" – that unit suffers a single hit with a Strength and AP equal to that of the initial shot. If there is no unengaged enemy unit within 6", then the Wound is still saved, but the shot is not redirected. This does not cause templates or blast markers to be repositioned.

> 'Only the deathless can truly comprehend the burden of unfailing loyalty.'
> *- Vargard Obyron of the Sautekh Dynasty*

DEATHMARKS

For countless millennia, Deathmark Squads have served the Necrons nobility as snipers and assassins. Even when they were beings of flesh and blood, Deathmarks had a reputation for cold-hearted precision and patience. Now, housed in tireless metal bodies, Deathmarks are more deadly than they ever were in the Time of Flesh.

Whilst Deathmarks are as much part of a Tomb World's army as Immortals and Necron Warriors, tradition dictates strict rules concerning their use. As agents of assassination and ambush, ancient codes forbid the deployment of Deathmarks in wars between the nobility, or against other 'honourable' enemies. Fortunately, as most alien foes are considered far from worthy until they have had a chance to prove otherwise on the battlefield, and few enemy commanders encounter Deathmarks and live to tell the tale, this gives all but the most traditional and hidebound nemesors carte blanche to employ these assassins against pretty much any alien he sees fit. An honourable corpse is still a corpse, after all, and little given to benefiting from its a newly accorded status.

Deathmarks seldom take position with the rest of the army at battle's start. Instead, they slip sideways out of reality and monitor the ongoing conflict from a hyperspace oubliette – a pocket dimension riding the gap between then and now. They can remain here for days upon end, waiting patiently for the opportune moment to act. Deathmarks choose their time of intercession carefully. They can be summoned to the fray at the order of the army's commander, but more often they are left to employ their own judgement – biotransference has done little to dull the Deathmarks' predatory instincts and most nemesors are content to trust to this. From their hyperspace sanctuary, the Deathmarks can track the initiation and target points of enemy communication channels, teleport beams and even orbital descents with childish ease. Thus are the deployment locations of enemy commanders and reinforcements betrayed.

With the target tracked and established, the Deathmarks exit their oubliette to appear silently upon a ridge or ruin that affords unobstructed view of their quarry. From here, the Deathmarks place the hunter's mark from which they take their name – an eerie green energy halo that plays about the target's head. The halo glows brightly through five dimensions, ensuring that no matter how far or by what manner the target flees, the Deathmarks will never lose track of him. Naturally, such a marking does not last forever, perhaps only an hour or so at best, but an hour is a laughably long time for a Deathmark squad on the hunt. The target will be lucky to survive more than a few seconds before being torn apart by fire from the Deathmarks' long-barrelled synaptic disintegrators.

	WS	BS	S	T	W	I	A	Ld	Sv
Deathmark	4	4	4	4	1	2	1	10	3+

UNIT TYPE: Infantry.

WARGEAR:
Synaptic disintegrator: This rifle fires a compressed leptonic beam that destroys synaptic tissue.

Range	Str	AP	Type
24"	X	5	Rapid Fire, Sniper

SPECIAL RULES: Deep Strike, Reanimation Protocols.

Ethereal Interception: Immediately after an enemy unit arrives from reserve, any Deathmark units in Deep Strike reserve that have not yet entered play can themselves choose to enter play via Deep Strike, usually in the enemy turn. Any Deathmark units that choose not to enter play in this fashion make reserve rolls as normal in subsequent turns.

Hunters from Hyperspace: When a Deathmark unit deploys, choose a non-vehicle enemy unit on the battlefield (even a unit in a transport) to be their prey – place a counter next to the chosen unit to serve as a reminder. Any Deathmark unit that shoots at, or strikes blows against, a unit marked in this fashion will score a Wound on a roll of 2+.

'Once you are marked, there is no escape.'

- Illic Nightspear
Master of Pathfinders

FLAYED ONE PACKS

Flayed Ones are carrion creatures, the victims of a terrible madness that took root during the last days of the War in Heaven. Their curse was the parting gift of one of the C'tan: Llandu'gor, the Flayer. It is said that when the Necrons turned upon the C'tan, the Flayer was not merely splintered as were his brothers, but utterly obliterated. Yet, in his dying moments, he called down a terrible curse upon his betrayers, tainting them with an echo of his fearsome hunger. For aeons the Flayer's curse went unnoticed and unseen. By the time the madness began to manifest, the afflicted Necrons had travelled far and wide, unwittingly spreading the disease to countless worlds.

A Necron over whom the flayer curse has taken hold suffers a slow and tortuous erosion of sanity. It begins to revel in the bloody ruin of fleshed foes, and is driven to claim gruesome trophies of skin, sinew and bone. As the madness progresses, the victim becomes compelled to feast upon the fallen. It cannot actually digest or consume flesh in any sense – the blood simply seeps through the gaps in its exoskeleton to clog its joints and pool at its feet – yet still the Necron is driven to gorge itself upon gore in a doomed attempt to sate an unquenchable lust. Physical changes occur shortly thereafter, wracking and twisting the afflicted Necron's form into something as warped in body as it is in protocol and function. Ultimately, the accursed Necron simply disappears, drawn by unknown instinct to a pocket dimension beyond ours, where he will forever dwell amidst the charnel palaces of the Flayed Ones.

Other Necrons loathe the Flayed Ones and fear them for the disease they carry. As a result, those suspected of infection are banished or destroyed before the affliction becomes contagious. However, no manner of precaution can prevent a pack of Flayed Ones joining a battle already underway. They can materialise at any time, lured from their bleak dimension by the scent of blood and carnage. Flayed Ones commonly attack with little regard for strategy, though they will occasionally have the presence of mind not to attack immediately, stalking their target until it is vulnerable. This is best done from downwind, as Flayed Ones are wreathed in a dense stench of rotting flesh. When the moment to attack comes, Flayed Ones strike without hesitation, slashing at their prey with twisted talons and keening shrill madness. If the enemy flees, Flayed Ones rarely pursue, choosing instead to feast upon their victims. However, if the enemy proves particularly resilient, the Flayed Ones inevitably retreat, skittering into the shadows to await a more tractable target.

Most Overlords make little or no attempt to adapt their plans for the unwanted actions of Flayed Ones, preferring rather to accept any advantage their presence brings. Regardless of the Flayed Ones' usefulness, it is not uncommon for an Overlord to order the execution of any surviving Flayed Ones at battle's end. Alas, only the most insane are slaughtered easily. The rest slip sideways through the dimensions to reappear in their palaces of rotting flesh, laden with their newly-claimed trophies and reeking of fresh blood.

	WS	BS	S	T	W	I	A	Ld	Sv
Flayed One	4	1	4	4	1	2	3	10	4+

UNIT TYPE: Infantry.

SPECIAL RULES: Deep Strike, Infiltrate, Reanimation Protocols.

'Through technology we thought to defeat the natural order. But the onset of eternity cannot be denied forever; the universe will see us humbled for our presumption.

'Yet its methods of attack are limited. We long ago removed our bodies from mortality's grasp and bartered away our souls for technological baubles and the trappings of power. Our minds, then, are all that remains for us to lose, and it is here that the next stroke against us will fall.

'Though our individual afflictions may take different forms, sooner or later we will all be lost to madness.'

- Szarekh, Last of the Silent Kings

TRIARCH PRAETORIANS

In the Necron dynasties, the Praetorians held the responsibility of maintaining the Triarch's rule, to ensure that wars and politics alike were pursued according to ancient codes. As such, they acted outside the political structures, and held both the right and the means to enforce their will should a Lord, Overlord or even a Phaeron's behaviour contravene the edicts of old. However, the Triarch Praetorians also held a higher responsibility: to ensure that the Necron dynasties never fell, that their codes of law and order did not vanish into the darkness. In this, they failed. To all intents and purposes, the War in Heaven saw the destruction of the Necron dynasties. Though the Triarch Praetorians fought at the forefront of that cataclysm, their efforts were not enough. That shame hung heavy on the survivors and drove them to forsake hibernation. As the final sparks of the War in Heaven burnt out, the last Triarch Praetorians withdrew to the Necrontyr's ancient seats of power on the northern rim, preserving what they could from the vengeance of the Eldar.

From their concealed fortresses, the Triarch Praetorians plotted for that day, many millennia distant though it was, when the Necrons would emerge to dominate the galaxy once again, when the laws of old would once more hold sway. Yet they knew there was a good chance that the untested stasis technology would fail, and that their sleeping kin would never wake. So it was that the Triarch Praetorians came to travel widely throughout the galaxy, masquerading as grim-visaged gods on countless primitive worlds. They brought the codes of the Necrontyr to credulous primitives, reshaping cultures according to their own ideals. Few civilisations wholly embraced the Triarch Praetorians' teachings; many more were exterminated by wars, natural disaster or the vengeful outriders of Alaitoc Craftworld, who were ever determined to see the Triarch Praetorians fail in their mission. Nonetheless, fragments of Triarch lore and archeotech survive on worlds not trod upon by Necrons in many thousands of years.

Now, as the Necrons stir ever more into wakefulness, the Triarch Praetorians have sensed an opportunity to expunge their failure. They are travelling across the galaxy, Tomb World to Tomb World, rebinding the sundered pieces of the Necron dynasties. It will be a long and interminably slow process, for the galaxy is vast beyond imagining, and the locations of many Necron worlds have been lost, but the Triarch Praetorians have patience enough for the search and a burning determination to see it done. Once a Tomb World has been contacted and bound into the newly-founded dynasties, a host of Triarch Praetorians is assigned to that world in perpetuity, to govern its protocols and act in its defence. So it is that formations of Triarch Praetorians are often found at a battle's forefront in the defence against invaders and campaigns of reclamation alike. Even could he do so, no noble would refuse such assistance, for extreme age has little dulled a Triarch Praetorian squad's combat skills.

Triarch Praetorians seldom fight in a battle's initial waves, preferring to hover above the fray on gravity displacement packs. From here they watch carefully, not only for the moment at which their intercession will have the most impact, but also to observe the foe's actions. Though Triarch Praetorians share the usual Necron contempt for any race that is not their own, they are ever watchful for an opponent marked millennia ago by their influence, and sometimes proclaim such creatures honourable foes against whom the codes of battle must be observed. This can prove frustrating to an army's commander – such niceties are unwelcome impedance to the battle's prosecution – but it would be a bold nemesor indeed who overruled the wishes of a Triarch Praetorian in so blatant a fashion.

	WS	BS	S	T	W	I	A	Ld	Sv
Triarch Praetorian	4	4	5	5	1	2	1	10	3+

UNIT TYPE: Jump Infantry.

WARGEAR:
Rod of covenant: A blast from a rod of covenant can reduce even a Necron to a smouldering pool of fused metal – organic creatures simply explode into clouds of flaming ash.

In addition to being a power weapon in close combat, a rod of covenant is a shooting weapon with the following profile:

Range	Str	AP	Type
6"	5	2	Assault 1

SPECIAL RULES: Fearless, Reanimation Protocols.

TRIARCH STALKERS

Like an enormous mechanical spider, a Triarch Stalker looms over the battlefield with its multiple slicing limbs and devastating weaponry controlled by a high-ranking Triarch Praetorian. When a Triarch Stalker advances, it does so with a speed and surety that belies its jerking gait. Indeed, it can cover all manner of terrain with a deftness and precision seldom found in the walkers of less advanced races.

While the Triarch Stalker can mount a wide array of anti-infantry and anti-armour weaponry, it is most commonly employed as a dedicated tank-hunter that roams far ahead of the main army. Able to navigate dense jungle and mountainous terrain as swiftly and sure-footedly as open plains, Triarch Stalkers can easily outmanoeuvre more cumbersome tracked vehicles, the better to unleash their withering firepower against the thinner armour presented by the target's flanks and rear. As such attacks are much more effective when the enemy is taken unawares, Triarch Stalkers rarely indulge in sustained fusillades. Instead, they prefer to employ hit and run tactics, launching one or two salvoes of fire and then skittering away into the shadows before the enemy can react to their threat.

On those occasions when a Triarch Stalker is deployed in the heart of the Necron battle lines, its main function is to provide close fire support, and it is typically equipped with a heat ray – a multipurpose fusion weapon. If an enemy tank stalls the attack, one focussed blast from the Triarch Stalker's heat ray is sufficient to end the threat. Similarly, if dug-in enemy infantry is hampering the Necron advance, a Triarch Stalker can break the deadlock. The pilot simply sets the heat ray to dispersed beam, and sends clouds of scorching plasma swirling into every crevasse to broil the enemy alive.

Should the Triarch Stalker's firepower prove insufficient to the task at hand, it can instruct nearby Necron phalanxes to add their firepower to its own, and even transmit targeting data to ensure these augmentative volleys are as accurate as possible. Only the toughest and bravest of foes can withstand such a barrage – others are driven screaming from the battlefield, or mown down by the pinpoint salvoes.

Such a difference does a Triarch Stalker's presence make that habitual foes of the Necrons have learnt to prioritise its destruction. To guard against this, each Triarch Stalker is protected by layered quantum shielding. Though a determined assault can still breach these energy fields, it normally buys the Triarch Stalker enough time to withdraw. With their durability thus enhanced, Triarch Stalkers are increasingly deployed at the head of vanguard forces, there to bear the brunt of the enemy's counterattack until the main body of the Necron army reaches the battle zone.

> 'Excellent! The Triarch Stalkers have come. Now there shall be a reckoning with our arrogant inferiors.'
>
> – Nemesor Zahndrekh of the Sautekh Dynasty,
> Regent of the Crownworld of Gidrim

	WS	BS	S	Armour F	Armour S	Armour R	I	A
Triarch Stalker	4	4	7	11	11	11	2	3

UNIT TYPE: Vehicle, Open-topped, Walker.

WARGEAR: Quantum shielding.

Heat ray: The heat ray can be fired in either a focussed or dispersed beam. Choose which you wish to use before the Triarch Stalker makes its shooting attack.

Focussed Beam

Range	Strength	AP	Type
24"	8	1	Heavy 2, Melta

Dispersed Beam

Range	Strength	AP	Type
Template	5	4	Heavy 1

SPECIAL RULES: Living Metal, Move Through Cover.

Targeting Relay: If a Triarch Stalker shoots at an enemy unit and manages at least one hit, place a counter or coin next to the target. All other friendly units that shoot at the same target later in the same Shooting phase count their weapons as twin-linked.

C'TAN SHARDS

C'tan Shards are all that remain of the once mighty star-gods. They are echoes of their former selves, splinters of energy that survived the Necrons' betrayal and were enslaved in turn. Most now languish in unbreakable servitude to their former vassals, utterly incapable of acting without commission. Should a C'tan Shard rebel, or a fault develop in its control relays, then fail-safe mechanisms automatically activate, whisking the creature back to its tomb, there to languish for centuries until times are dire enough that its services must be called upon again. Even with these precautions, the Necrons are wary of employing C'tan Shards in battle. Though the chance of escape is remote, the possibility remains, so the day must be dark indeed before the tesseract labyrinths are opened and the C'tan unleashed upon the galaxy once again.

Even in their reduced and wholly fettered state, C'tan Shards are beings of near-unlimited power. They can manifest energy blasts, control the minds of lesser beings, manipulate the flow of time, and banish foes to alternate realities. Indeed, a C'tan Shard's abilities are limited only by two things: its imagination – which is immense – and glimmering memories of the being from which it was severed. Whilst no individual C'tan Shard has full recall of the omnipotent creature it once was, each carries the personality and hubris of that far vaster and more puissant being. Though a C'tan Shard has the power to reduce a tank to molten slag with but a gesture, it might simply not occur to it to do so, as its gestalt primogenitor would have tackled the situation through other means, such as by devolving the crew into primordial ooze, or deceiving them into attacking their own allies. The only hope of defeating a C'tan is to breach its necrodermis – the living metal form that cages its essence. If the necrodermis is compromised, the C'tan Shard explodes in a pulse of blinding energy, its being scattered to the galactic winds.

Whilst it is true that many C'tan Shards are now indentured to Necron service, this by no means accounts for the entire pantheon. Rumours of C'tan-like beings can be found across the galaxy, though many are merely entities that exhibit inexplicable powers. Indeed, any such being – whether Warp-spawned Daemon, energy-based life form or an alien with advanced technology – can be mistaken for a C'tan if the observer is primitive, credulous or simply ill-informed enough. This discrepant information causes great confusion concerning the exact number and nature of the surviving C'tan, even among the Eldar. Records held in the Black Library contradict those maintained on Ulthwé, which are again at odds with the archives held on Alaitoc. There might be four C'tan, four thousand or any number in between. However, all Eldar agree that the splinters of knowledge held by the Imperium are so flawed and confused that they, if anything, move further from the truth with each fresh discovery made. Any who go looking for proof of a C'tan's existence can easily uncover it, but this speaks more to the mindset of the searcher than it does to any value of the 'evidence'.

	WS	BS	S	T	W	I	A	Ld	Sv
C'tan Shard	5	5	7	7	4	4	4	10	4+

UNIT TYPE: Monstrous Creature (Character).

WARGEAR:
Necrodermis: C'tan Shards are bound by a living metal necrodermis which both protects and contains their essence.

C'tan Shards have a 4+ invulnerable save. If the C'tan Shard loses its last Wound, models within D6" of the C'tan Shard suffer a Strength 4, AP 1 hit.

SPECIAL RULES: Fearless, Eternal Warrior.

Immune to Natural Law: C'tan Shards ignore the effects of difficult and dangerous terrain while moving.

"They came to us as gods and we, like fools, took them at their word. Mephet'ran the Deceiver, Aza'gorod the Nightbringer, Iash'uddra the Endless Swarm; I curse their names, and the names of all their malevolent brethren.'
- from the Chronicle of Szarekh, Last of the Silent Kings

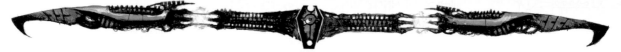

C'TAN MANIFESTATIONS OF POWER

C'tan Shards are beings of reality-warping power. Their abilities are many and varied, often harking back to those their parent-entities enjoyed. A C'tan Shard always has two of the following abilities, selected at the points cost presented in the army list (see page 92). Note that each ability can be taken only once in an army.

ENTROPIC TOUCH
Metal decays on contact with the C'tan Shard's rotten grasp.

The C'tan Shard's close combat attacks have the Entropic Strike special rule.

GAZE OF DEATH
Eyes blazing with dark energy, the C'tan Shard drains the life from all in the vicinity.

In the Assault phase, after all other blows in the C'tan Shard's combat have been struck, centre the large blast marker on the C'tan Shard. All other models beneath the marker (friend or foe) suffer a Strength 3 hit with no armour saves allowed. If the C'tan Shard causes one or more unsaved Wounds in this manner, it regains one Wound lost earlier in the battle. These Wounds do not count towards combat resolution.

GRAND ILLUSION
The C'tan Shard weaves a glamour of deception, preventing the foe from seeing the true disposition of the Necron forces.

After all forces have been deployed and all Scout moves have been made, roll a D3. You can immediately redeploy this many friendly units, subject to the normal deployment rules for the mission. This power can be used to move units into, or out of, reserve.

LORD OF FIRE
This C'tan Shard is a creature of living flame, able to command the fires wielded by the enemy.

All flamer weapons (as well as heat rays, burnas, skorchas, inferno cannons and any weapon described as using 'flame' or 'fire' as its effect or in its special rules) and weapons with the melta type fired within 12" of the C'tan Shard have a chance of exploding. Roll a D6 each time such a weapon is fired within range. On a roll of a 1, the weapon detonates. If carried by a non-vehicle model, the model is removed from play as a casualty. If mounted on a vehicle, it counts as a weapon destroyed result. In either case, the shot(s) are lost.

MOULDER OF WORLDS
Tortured rock buckles and heaves, showering the C'tan Shard's foes with boulders.

This power is a shooting attack with the following profile:

Range	Strength	AP	Type
24"	4	-	Assault 1, Large Blast

PYRESHARDS
The C'tan Shard conjures specks of blazing black matter and directs them against its foes.

This power is a shooting attack with the following profile:

Range	Strength	AP	Type
18"	4	-	Assault 8

SENTIENT SINGULARITY
The C'tan Shard's presence destabilises gravitational forces, disrupting engines, teleport beams and warp jumps.

All enemy vehicles within 6" of the C'tan Shard treat all terrain as dangerous (if a vehicle starts its movement more than 6" away from the C'tan Shard, test as soon as the vehicle moves to within 6" of the C'tan Shard). Additionally, Deep Striking enemy units attempting to arrive within 6" of the C'tan Shard automatically suffer a Deep Strike mishap if their scatter roll is a double (whether or not a hit was rolled).

SWARM OF SPIRIT DUST
A cloud of swirling darkness conceals the C'tan Shard from the gaze of his foes.

The C'tan Shard is treated as having assault and defensive grenades. Furthermore it has the Stealth special rule.

TIME'S ARROW
Mutating the flow of causation and remoulding the temporal stream, the C'tan Shard casts its foe back into the darkness from before time was time.

At the start of the Assault phase, after assault moves have been made but before blows are struck, nominate one enemy model in base contact with the C'tan Shard (if there are any). That model must pass an Initiative test or be removed as a casualty with no saves of any kind allowed.

TRANSDIMENSIONAL THUNDERBOLT
The C'tan Shard projects a bolt of crackling energy from its outstretched palm.

This power is a shooting attack with the following profile:

Range	Strength	AP	Type
24"	9	2	Assault 1

WRITHING WORLDSCAPE
The natural world revolts at the C'tan Shard's presence, the very ground writhing and shaking as the physical laws holding reality together are undone.

Whilst the C'tan Shard is on the battlefield, all difficult terrain is also dangerous for the enemy. If the terrain is already dangerous, the Dangerous Terrain test is failed on a 1 or 2.

TOMB BLADES

The Tomb Blade was originally designed as a spacefighter during the final days of the War in Heaven. As Necrons' robotic bodies are immune to the hazards of interplanetary space, traditional pressure-sealed and canopied craft were unnecessary from the very outset. Acting in swarms that were dozens or even hundreds strong, Tomb Blades would swarm over enemy capital ships, overwhelming armour and weapon systems with waves of pinpoint gauss and tesla fire. So successfully did the craft perform in its primary environment that modified versions soon appeared in planet side battles – one of the few occasions in which the hidebound traditions of the Necron military were adapted to better exploit emergent opportunity.

The Tomb Blade has a curious motion for a craft of its design, eschewing the arrow-straight attack vectors of other jetbikes and fighter craft. The Tomb Blade's dimensional repulsor engines ensure that gravity, momentum and other forces have little purchase upon its frame. As a result, the craft often corkscrews across the battlefield rather than taking a more direct approach, and constantly changes vector and altitude in a manner fit to boggle the enemy's aim. No flesh and blood pilot could ever hope to contend with such an anarchic approach without succumbing to blackouts and nausea, but such hazards have no hold over machines.

Despite appearances to the contrary, the attack patterns performed by Tomb Blades are strictly controlled by a series of hyper-fractal equations. Indeed, they have to be, for a Necron Warrior alone would make for a truly dreadful pilot. To compensate for this, attack patterns are entirely pre-planned and the pilot cannot alter them once in flight, though it can switch between different tactical packages in order to adapt to fresh objectives.

The pre-programmed nature of a Tomb Blade's flight means that it is therefore theoretically possible to predict the flight path it will take, but only a genius-level intellect could divine that there was a pattern at all. Even if said genius could isolate and identify the particular set of equations in use, no conventional targeting computer could ever hope to process the data fast enough to be of any use. Thus, a Tomb Blade is just as difficult a quarry as the most accomplished of all mortals, even though its pilot's skill is immensely inferior.

Tomb Blades often operate far ahead of the main army, striking at lightly defended positions, supply convoys and other targets of opportunity. Though the planet side craft do not mount the starship-busting weaponry of the spacefighter variants, the twin-linked tesla carbines and gauss blasters can prove just as devastating when employed against advancing infantry. Such is the Tomb Blade's unpredictable advance that the piercing whine of its dimensional repulsors is often the only clue to its approach. At that point, astute enemies dive for any cover they can find. The others disintegrate as the air around them explodes in a blaze of unstable energy.

	WS	BS	S	T	W	I	A	Ld	Sv
Tomb Blade	4	4	4	4(5)	1	2	1	10	4+

UNIT TYPE: Jetbike.

WARGEAR: Twin-linked tesla carbine.

SPECIAL RULES: Reanimation Protocols.

UPGRADES:

Shadowloom: *This scarab-sized generator projects an aura of darkness about the Tomb Blade.*

A model with a shadowloom has the Stealth special rule.

Nebuloscope: *This arcane device allows the Tomb Blade's pilot to track his prey through seven different dimensions, allowing for a much more accurate shot.*

A model with a nebuloscope has a Ballistic Skill of 5.

Shield vanes: *Many Tomb Blades run with additional armour panels, increasing their durability by a small, but significant, amount.*

A model with shield vanes has an armour save of 3+.

NECRON DESTROYERS

Destroyers are the deranged agents of annihilation whose sole reason for existence is centred around an unshakeable yearning to quench the flames of life. A Destroyer cares not for borders or allegiance, nor does he make any distinction between the innocent and the damned – all life is his enemy, and all living creatures are his prey.

It is not the Destroyers' violent madness alone that makes them so different from the other denizens of a Tomb World. Insanity infects many a slumbering Necron, though it rarely takes a dramatic form, but instead merely exacerbates the victim's innate eccentricities. Yet even the lowliest Necron Warrior longs for a return to Time of Flesh, and because its physical form is all that now echoes the living, breathing, soulful creature it once was, it will under no circumstances tolerate further dilution or corruption of that physical form. Instead, for a Destroyer, everything is subsumed into the all-important goal of annihilation. They ruthlessly adapt, augment or expunge any facet of their physical form if it will improve their mission of slaughter. Legs are removed in favour of repulsor platforms, arms are fused to the workings of gauss cannons. Even the Destroyer's senses are reconfigured to better serve target lock and prediction capability, its neural circuitry repathed to improve response times at the cost of vestigial emotions. None of this is to say that Destroyers do not feel fear; though they might explain a retreat away as conserving resources, it is a retreat nonetheless, spurred on by a spark of self-preservation that will never quite be extinguished.

What makes the rise of the Destroyers truly disturbing is that they can be found on almost every Tomb World, from the poorest fringeworld to the noblest of crownworlds. This suggests that the descent into this particular form of madness is driven by subconscious imperative – possibly one implanted by the C'tan during biotransference. This does not mean that Destroyers hail from every level of Necron society. It takes a certain freedom of personality to embrace nihilism with such cold-blooded determination, a level of individuality denied to low-ranking Necrons. Destroyers therefore, almost without exception, emerge from the ranks of Immortals, Lychguard and, occasionally, Deathmarks. Most are banished to the outskirts of their Tomb World, dwelling in isolated fortresses ruled over by courts of Destroyer Lords.

A Destroyer's chilling dedication to destruction is a valuable addition to any Necron army. On most campaigns, their brutal efficiency more than compensates for the almost habitual insubordination with which they treat other Necrons of all ranks. The canniest and most thorough nemesors make a direct point of building campaigns around the actions of Destroyers, rather than making doomed attempts to enforce their own battle plan on the twisted warriors. So long as a Destroyer knows that there are other forms of life in the vicinity, it will direct its baleful attention upon their destruction, and has no intellect or focus to spare for such irrelevancies as orders and strategy. Once the enemy is in sight, Destroyers pay little or no heed to their allies, but instead settle into optimised and self-sufficient extermination patterns: shattering enemy formations with long range salvoes of gauss fire before moving into point-blank range to methodically scour survivors from the blackened craters.

	WS	BS	S	T	W	I	A	Ld	Sv
Necron Destroyer	4	4	4	5	1	2	1	10	3+
Heavy Destroyer	4	4	4	5	1	2	1	10	3+

UNIT TYPE: Jump Infantry.

WARGEAR: Gauss cannon (Destroyer only), heavy gauss cannon (Heavy Destroyer only).

SPECIAL RULES: Preferred Enemy (Everything!), Reanimation Protocols.

'The Destroyers? They are weapons, nothing more, and should be expended as such. They are Necron in form only, having been reborn to a madness deeper than any other to which I have borne witness. Whilst I hold nothing but approval for their drive and efficiency, I can present no logic adequate to justify their ultimate goal. A warrior's proper function is to fight for a profound objective, to leave behind works or deeds greater than himself. Given free reign, the Destroyers would leave behind nothing; not life, nor art, nor glory. Only dust would remain. I am a soulless machine, yet even I feel pity for their victims.'

- Szarekh, Last of the Silent Kings

The Army of Aeons Past

CANOPTEK WRAITHS

While a Tomb World fitfully slumbers, Canoptek Wraiths are its eyes and ears. They flit silently through the dusty halls, patrolling for intruders and inspecting systems for damage and decay. The Wraiths are primarily probe mechanoids, programmed to report back to their Canoptek Spyder controllers via interstitial interface, rather than to act under their own cognisance. When orders are received, the Wraith carries them out with unfaltering resolve. Be it commanded to strike against an intruder, or conduct repairs in the heart of a collapsing tomb, the Wraith will follow instructions to completion, or to the termination of its function.

The Canoptek Wraith's most notable feature is its dimensional destabilisation matrix – a phase shifter that allows it to skip in and out of reality. It can even adjust the modulation of the matrix in order to keep sections of its form in different states. Whilst a completely phased-out existence can be sustained almost indefinitely, a half-phased state takes a great deal of energy to sustain. Indeed, the Wraith's body is little more than a series of interlocking power generators and etherium lode conduits, and even so it can exist in dual state for only limited periods of time.

The dimensional destabilisation matrix was originally conceived to allow the Wraiths to reach into and repair solid machinery without all the trouble of removing outer components or armoured casings. It is, however, no less valuable when dealing with intruders – if the timing is correct, a Canoptek Wraith can phase its claws and tendrils inside an opponent, swiftly resolidifying them to sever arteries, nerve clusters and other vital pathways without leaving an external mark to show for it. Furthermore, the foe must time his return blows with great care, lest his weapons pass through the Canoptek Wraith's phased-out form.

Though their primary function is to watch over their sleeping masters, Wraiths are often drafted into armies to serve as advance scouts. The dimensional destabilisation matrix allows a Wraith to traverse all manner of terrain without pause and also serves to hide it from enemy eyes and sensors. Many an enemy army has advanced across a Tomb World, little knowing that its every move is watched, recorded and reported on by the ghostly Canoptek Wraith. Only the most observant of foes can hope to catch sight of the lurking Wraith's spectral form or detect the unsettling electronic chatter that accompanies its precise transmissions. Even then, such things are commonly dismissed as tricks of the imagination.

Once the inevitable battle begins, the Canoptek Wraith is then tasked with sowing terror and disorder throughout the enemy ranks by striking at commanders, support troops and supply lines – anything that a more conventional strike force would struggle to reach. Indeed, sometimes an enemy commander won't even make it to the battle. Instead he is slain in his sleep the night before by the cold claws of a Canoptek Wraith assassin to whom doors, guards and force fields are no barrier.

	WS	BS	S	T	W	I	A	Ld	Sv
Canoptek Wraith	4	4	6	4	2	2	3	10	3+

UNIT TYPE: Jump Infantry.

WARGEAR: Phase shifter.

SPECIAL RULES: Fearless.

Phase Attacks: Close combat attacks made by Canoptek Wraiths have the Rending special rule.

Wraithflight: Canoptek Wraiths are never slowed by Difficult Terrain, and automatically pass Dangerous Terrain tests.

UPGRADES:

Whip coils: Some Canoptek Wraiths are equipped with writhing mechanical tendrils that constrict around the foe, pinning them in place whilst other weapons do their bloody work.

Whilst any enemy model is in base contact with a model with whip coils they count their Initiative value as 1, regardless of their actual Initiative value.

CANOPTEK SCARABS

Canoptek Scarabs are constructs, designed to break down organic and non-organic matter into raw energy. This harvested energy can then be woven into fresh forms at the direction of the Scarabs' controller. In the confines of a tomb, this invariably involves stripping down destroyed or damaged components which can then be reborn as replacement parts, or else as further Canoptek Spyders, Scarabs or Wraiths to oversee and manage the tomb's functions. Almost anything can be replicated in this fashion, providing that the wellspring of energy is sufficient to the task at hand. Given time, a suitably large swarm of Scarabs can consume an entire hive city, and all its inhabitants, thereafter using the purloined energies to create anything from a battlefleet to a fully functioning Necron tomb ready for habitation.

With their swift, darting movements and high-pitched chittering, Canoptek Scarabs appear to mimic the behaviours of organic invertebrates. However, they lack for a true hive mind. A swarm of Scarabs has no more intelligence than one Scarab alone – which is to say none at all – and is driven by simple instructions and even simpler instincts.

Essentially mindless feeding machines, Canoptek Scarabs are typically controlled by interstitial carrier waves from Canoptek Spyders or Crypteks. If this signal is disrupted or jammed, Canoptek Scarabs simply revert to their most basic instincts and devour anything in the immediate vicinity – even other Scarabs or Necrons. However, the interstitial interfaces are incredibly difficult to detect, let alone disrupt. Should the controlling entity be destroyed, another automatically assumes control within moments. Even if the enemy can completely remove the carrier waves, this often creates a far greater problem than before. The Canoptek Scarabs will no longer operate under the Necrons' direct control, and as part of their reversion to base programming they will expend any accumulated energy on fashioning ever more Scarabs, thus creating a voracious self-replicating swarm that only something of the order of saturation bombardment has any hope of exterminating.

An Overlord will often begin a battle by unleashing a swarm of Canoptek Scarabs, hoping that the foe will waste much-needed ammunition blasting the scavengers apart before the true assault is launched. Indeed, a particularly canny Overlord can determine the resolve of various enemy formations by how they react. Hardened troops will see the Scarabs for the slight threat they are, destroying or driving them off with disciplined volleys. Others enemies will be driven mad with fear by the pervasive drone of the swarm's wings, or even overwhelmed and devoured by the chittering tide. Either way, an observant Overlord can glean valuable information as to where the strongest pockets of resistance lie and plan his attacks accordingly.

However, where Canoptek Scarabs truly come into their own is when unleashed upon tanks and other vehicles. Once a Scarab has latched onto a hull, it begins to feed, breaking down the victim's armour plating and leaving it vulnerable to attacks from other sources. If not quickly destroyed or driven away, a swarm of Canoptek Scarabs can even burrow their way through the hull, turning a mighty engine of war into a horror-filled prison for its soon-to-be devoured crew.

	WS	BS	S	T	W	I	A	Ld	Sv
Canoptek Scarabs	2	2	3	3	3	2	4	10	5+

UNIT TYPE: Beasts.

SPECIAL RULES: Entropic Strike, Fearless, Swarms.

> Take my advice: if you hear the chittering of Scarab wings, just run, and keep running 'til the sound is gone. Don't stop, and don't look back. If one of your squadmates starts screaming, it's because the Scarabs are on him, and you'll die right alongside if you try to help.
>
> I'm not saying you'll be able to outrun the devils, mind. Even goin' full pelt and with a head start, you'll lose ground pretty quickly. Best you can hope for is that you can run quicker than the rest of your squad; but then no one ever said life in the Imperial Guard was fair.'
>
> - *Quartermaster Kross, Cadian 312th, Executed for dishonourable conduct 777.M41*

CANOPTEK SPYDERS

Unlike their Necron masters, Canoptek Spyders never sleep, but wile away the aeons servicing the structures of their Tomb World. Even in their prime, these systems required constantly looped maintenance cycles lest they degraded beyond repair, and the withering centuries have only hastened this natural decay. It is a task both endless in scope and thankless in nature, but Canoptek Spyders are patient unto eternity.

Though it is essentially just an automated drone, a Canoptek Spyder is still a formidable foe when the situation demands. Its vast arrays of self-repair and backup systems, vital for enduring the uncaring millennia, offer substantial protection against a foe's weaponry. In return, any enemy foolish enough to stray within reach of the Canoptek Spyder will have flesh scoured from bone by an array of mechanical tools and pincers. As if this were not enough, each Canoptek Spyder will have a further selection of weaponry at its command, depending upon its function. Canoptek Spyders whose primary duties are oversight, rather than direct action, craft slaved hosts of Canoptek Scarabs and nanoscarabs within their abdomens, which are unleashed to effect repairs on nearby Necrons, or consume enemy weapons and armour. Others employ particle beam dissectors in place of claws and act as sentinels for the slumbering tomb.

Whilst Canoptek Spyders are not sentient by any strict definition, their complex and layered subroutines are incredibly resilient and can adapt to most situations. If a triad of Canoptek Spyders are operating in concert, one takes overall command, harnessing the processing capacity of the others to create a gestalt supermind far greater than the sum of its parts. This hyper-efficiency is passed on to all Canoptek Wraiths and Canoptek Scarabs in the immediate vicinity, allowing the Canoptek Spyders to affect a co-ordinated and precise response to any threat, be it a failed stasis-matrix or an enemy incursion. So it is that any intruders to a tomb are often slain before catching so much as a glimpse of a Necron, having already been overwhelmed by swarms of Scarabs and Wraiths silently directed by a looming Canoptek Spyder and ensuring the safety of their slumbering masters.

	WS	BS	S	T	W	I	A	Ld	Sv
Canoptek Spyder	3	3	6	6	3	2	2	10	3+

UNIT TYPE: Monstrous Creature.

WARGEAR:
Scarab hive: At the start of each Necron Movement phase, a Canoptek Spyder that is not locked in close combat can expend energy to create a Canoptek Scarab Swarm.

Nominate a Canoptek Scarab unit within 6" and roll a D6. On a roll of 2-6, add one base to the Canoptek Scarab unit – the base can move and act normally this turn. This can take the unit beyond its starting size. On a roll of a 1, the Scarab base is still placed, however, the Canoptek Spyder is drained by the energy expenditure and suffers a Wound with no armour or cover saves allowed. If the Scarab base cannot be placed for any reason, it is destroyed.

SPECIAL RULES: Fearless.

UPGRADES:
Fabricator claw array: The fabricator claw array is a close combat weapon. In addition, if a Canoptek Spyder with fabricator claws is in base contact with a damaged vehicle during the Shooting phase, it can attempt to repair one vehicle instead of making a shooting attack.

Roll a D6. If the result is 4 or more, then either a Weapon Destroyed result or Immobilised result (owning player's choice) is repaired. If a Weapon Destroyed result is repaired, that weapon can be fired in the Shooting phase of its next turn. The Canoptek Spyder cannot repair if it has gone to ground.

Gloom prism: The Gloom Prism's energy field creates a zone shrouded from Warp-spawned power.

Each time an enemy unit attempts to target the Canoptek Spyder, or a friendly unit within 3", with a psychic power, roll a D6 if the Psychic test is passed. On a 4+, the power is nullified and has no effect.

NECRON MONOLITHS

Nothing is so emblematic of Necron implacability than the Monolith. Like all Necron constructs, it is composed of living metal: a complex semi-sentient alloy that ripples and flows to repair damage in a blink of an eye. Target matrices and motive units, power conduits and command nodes – all are capable of comprehensive and near-instantaneous self repair. When combined with the vehicle's slab-sided armour plates, this makes the Monolith an incredibly daunting opponent for any enemy. Energy beams are absorbed and dispersed, whilst tank-busting missiles simply ricochet off the Monolith's armoured hide, leaving behind minor damage whose repair lies easily within the parameters of the living metal's arcane function. Indeed, the only way to truly halt the advance of a Monolith is to target it with a sustained period of focussed fire. Only by punching through the armoured shell to the vital systems and crew within can there be any hope of ending its threat. Few enemies, however, have the discipline to be so precise under fire, and even they must be swift in their targeting, lest they be disintegrated by the Monolith's formidable array of weaponry.

Even a single Monolith can muster enough firepower to be considered a small army in its own right. Most dramatic of its armaments is the particle whip, channelled through a glowing focus crystal atop the vehicle. A single ear-splitting discharge from the particle whip is enough to reduce tanks to smouldering wrecks and infantry to molecular vapour. Any enemies lucky enough to have survived will then have

to run the gauntlet of the Monolith's gauss flux arcs. These automated defence arrays rake the area around the Monolith in pre-programmed execution patterns, finely tuned to predict the panicked motions of foes under fire.

Yet the Monolith's greatest and most fearsome weapon is its eternity gate. This shimmering energy field is nothing less than a captive wormhole, bound into the very heart of the Monolith. With a simple mental command, the Monolith's crew can transform the eternity gate into a portal of exile, and those that fail to resist its pull are sucked out of reality entirely, banished forever to a temporal prison from which there can be no escape. Alternatively, the Monolith's crew can use the eternity gate as a form of dimensional corridor, pulling squads of Necrons from elsewhere on the battlefield, orbiting starships or even far-distant Tomb Worlds and deploying them to the Monolith's location. So is the Monolith rightly known as a forerunner to disaster, for where a Monolith teleports onto a planet's surface, an invading Necron army is rarely far behind...

			Armour		
	Type	BS	F	S	R
Necron Monolith	Heavy*, Skimmer, Tank	4	14	14	14

UNIT TYPE: Vehicle.

Heavy: *The vehicle cannot move faster than combat speed. When it shoots, it counts as having remained stationary.*

WARGEAR: Four gauss flux arcs, particle whip.

Eternity gate: The awesome energies of the eternity gate can be used in one of two ways in each of your turns, as a dimensional corridor or a portal of exile. The eternity gate cannot be destroyed separately from the Monolith.

- **Dimensional corridor:** At the start of the Movement phase, choose one friendly unengaged non-vehicle Necron unit on the battlefield or in reserve. That unit immediately phases out from its current position and 'disembarks' from the Monolith's portal. Any models that cannot be placed are removed as casualties, but the move is otherwise treated exactly as disembarking from a vehicle that has moved at combat speed.

- **Portal of exile:** The portal of exile is treated as a shooting attack. When used, all enemy models (not units) that are within D6" of the Monolith's portal, and have line of sight to it, must immediately pass a Strength test (models without a Strength value automatically pass) or be removed as a casualty with no saves of any kind allowed. Roll separately for each individual model.

Range	Strength	AP	Type
D6"	X	-	Heavy 1, Special

SPECIAL RULES: Deep Strike*, Living Metal.
* If a Monolith is held in reserve, it must arrive by Deep Strike.

The Army of Aeons Past

DOOMSDAY ARKS

Whatever personal eccentricities they might individually favour, all Overlords hold an absolute belief in victory through overwhelming firepower. Some of the Necrons' bitterest enemies have claimed this is simply due to the Necrons' android forms being somewhat less than impressive in swirling melee. However, the truth of the matter is that, as flesh and as machine, the Necrons have ever won their wars through the unrelenting application of superior technology. As such victories are invariably won at a distance, all Necron battle codicils emphasise ranged superiority. Nowhere is this more evident than in the Doomsday Ark, amongst the most feared of all weapons in the Necron arsenal.

In aspect, the Doomsday Ark appears deceptively fragile; its structure is skeletal and lacks the armour plates of more conventional battle vehicles. But to obsess on this apparent fragility is to overlook the Doomsday Ark's true purpose and potential. It is not a battle tank, intended to sit in the midst of a battle line, to give and receive punishing blows. Rather, the Doomsday Ark is nothing less than an enormous self-propelled doomsday cannon – a weapon that can win a battle with but a single shot. Any systems not directly pertaining to the Doomsday Ark's main armament are part of the motive units that propel it into position, or the shielding arrays that give it some measure of protection from enemy fire. Each of these secondary systems draws power from the same source as the doomsday cannon, and much of the pilot's concentration is taken up with ensuring that the energy distribution is appropriate to the tasks at hand.

The doomsday cannon itself is a wonder of super technology, easily eclipsing the primitive energy weapons of the Imperium. Even fired at low power the doomsday cannon is a fearsome weapon; when firing at full effect, its searing energy beams burn many times hotter than more conventional plasma weapons. Infantry caught in the doomsday cannon's fury are obliterated instantly; armoured vehicles reduced to glowing slag. In the face of a shot from a doomsday cannon, nothing less than a Titan's void shields can hope to offer anything more than a fool's hope of protection.

Unlike other vehicles, the Doomsday Ark relies little on either evasion or resilience for survival. Rather, its pilot's entire defensive strategy is one of pre-emptive strike – after all, enemies are infinitely less threatening once reduced to an expanding cloud of superheated energy. Thus does anything less than an overwhelming frontal assault on an Doomsday Ark inevitably end in disaster, the attackers vaporised long before their own weapons come into range. Nor do attempts to outflank serve any better. Though ponderous in advancing, the Doomsday Ark can be brought around to a new heading with surprising speed, emerald energy beams lancing out to slaughter its would-be destroyers.

| | Type | BS | Armour | | |
			F	S	R
Doomsday Ark	Open-topped, Skimmer	4	11	11	11

UNIT TYPE: Vehicle.

WARGEAR: Quantum shielding.

Two gauss flayer arrays: The Doomsday Ark has two separate arrays of five gauss flayers – one located along each flank – enabling it to 'broadside' enemy units. The two arrays can shoot at different targets to each other and the doomsday cannon, although all guns in the same array must shoot at the same target.

Doomsday cannon: For the doomsday cannon to be fired at full effect, the Doomsday Ark must remain stationary. The faster the Doomsday Ark moves, the more energy is directed away from the doomsday cannon.

Accordingly, the doomsday cannon has two profiles: one for if the Doomsday Ark remained stationary in the previous Movement phase and one for if it moved.

Stationary

Range	Strength	AP	Type
72"	9	1	Heavy 1, Large Blast

Combat Speed

Range	Strength	AP	Type
24"	7	4	Heavy 1, Blast

SPECIAL RULES: Living Metal.

ANNIHILATION BARGES

Annihilation Barges are the Necrons favoured anti-infantry support platforms. Each is armed with a linked pair of tesla destructors – enormous energy cannons that fire ferocious arcs of eldritch lightning. In the usual configuration of things, Annihilation Barges are set in fixed positions in the lowest and deepest sanctums of a Necron Tomb. Should an intruder manage to circumvent the layers of traps, service robots and prowling Necron Warriors, he will pass beneath the concealed emplacements in which the Annihilation Barges lie. An acrid discharge of emerald lightning later, and the interloper is naught but dust upon the tomb's stale breezes. When a Necron Overlord goes to war, the Annihilation Barges' ancient repulsor sleds are coaxed back into life and the vehicles add their firepower to the Tomb World's army.

Annihilation Barges are seldom swift enough to keep pace with even the ponderous advance of the Necron army – they are often deployed as defences for strategic locations. From here they can counter enemy scout elements, without facing the risk of being swept aside by a concerted attack. Not only does this render valuable sectors of the battlefield immune to all but the most determined of enemy assaults, it ensures that the Annihilation Barges themselves are guaranteed to find bloody purpose. Additionally, most Overlords task a squad of Immortals or Necron Warriors as guards. Such a partnership can prove advantageous for both parties – the Annihilation Barge has a screen of allies to drive back incoming assaults, whilst its bodyguard benefits from massive firepower.

The Annihilation Barge's tesla destructor is primarily an anti-personnel weapon, though only the most heavily-armoured tanks can risk its wrath with utter impunity. The tesla destructor employs much the same lightning-arc technology as found in the smaller tesla cannons and carbines. Its energy discharges wreak terrible harm on living targets, searing their flesh and boiling their blood. Furthermore, the bolts will often leap from target to target before they are finally grounded, leaving a trail of smouldering carnage across a broad swathe of the battlefield.

Nowhere are Annihilation Barges more commonly employed than on the northern frontier planets of the Akannazad dynasty. These Tomb Worlds are under perpetual assault from the Orks of Charadon, to whom the technology-rich and highly ordered Necron planets present an irresistible lure – both in terms of plunder and anarchic potential. Without resort to Annihilation Barges, many of these worlds would long ago been overrun. Few other weapons can wreak such efficient havoc amongst an oncoming Ork horde. The primary blast shreds the armour of Trukks and Looted Wagons, while the wildly arcing lightning incinerates any Ork Boyz unfortunate enough to be advancing alongside.

			Armour		
	Type	BS	F	S	R
Annihilation Barge	Open-topped, Skimmer	4	11	11	11

UNIT TYPE: Vehicle.

WARGEAR: Quantum shielding, tesla cannon, twin-linked tesla destructor.

SPECIAL RULES: Living Metal.

THE FALL OF THE TECHNOMANDRITES

Practically all of the Necrons' war machines owe provenance to a particular group of Crypteks: the Technomandrites of Magistrakh. This shadowy conclave stayed neutral during the First Wars of Secession, but sold their weaponeering knowledge to the highest bidder. The Technomandrites saw much profit from the spilt blood of their own kind, but it ultimately proved to be their undoing. When the Triarch's war against the Old Ones was first declared, the initial strike fell not against the aliens, but against Magistrakh. The reason the Silent King gave to the Necrontyr nobles was logical and compelling: if the Old Ones were to be defeated, no longer could one faction dictate the flow of arms. Yet this was, in part at least, a lie. Fear was the motivating force behind the Silent King's assault, fear that the Technomandrites' growing power would soon prove a challenge to the Triarch itself. Thus was the power of the Technomandrites broken forever. Those that remain are a but an echo of the past, and they dream of vengeance and restored glory.

DOOM SCYTHES

Doom Scythes are heralds of terror and dismay, supersonic fighter craft that range far ahead of a Necron invasion. Unlike many of the forces employed by the Necrons, Doom Scythes can function in a highly independent manner. Much of the craft's superstructure houses datastacks that are in turn heavily laden with strike plans, stratagems and tactical variants. When faced with a situation outside of known parameters, the pilot can sift through and retrieve the correct response from this datastack. Thanks to the ruthless precision of his android brain, the pilot can simulate billions of possible strategies in the span of a few nanoseconds.

Doom Scythes are often deployed to sap the resolve of the enemy before the battle proper begins, for its presence induces an almost irrational terror in living creatures. The Doom Scythe's primary propulsion system is an scaled up and augmented version of the dimensional repulsor drive employed on Tomb Blades. On those smaller craft, the whine of the drive is piercing and discomforting. On a Doom Scythe, the scale and amplitude of the sound is many hundreds of times greater; it resonates deep within the primitive core of living brains, playing havoc with memory, perception and sanity. Victims collapse into catatonia, slump into slack-jawed vacuity and suffer hallucinations of their dead comrades returned to worm-eaten life. Little wonder is it then that entire armies of battle-tested veterans have been known to throw down their weapons and flee at a Doom Scythe's onset, or else gouge out their own eyes in futile attempts to stem the images scratching at their senses.

Should the foe not yield the battle on the Doom Scythe's first pass, its pilot will then unleash the full fury of his craft's firepower. Tesla destructors explode into life, raking the battlefield with arcs of eldritch lightning, instantly incinerating any infantry not cowering in cover. Armoured targets can perhaps weather this sizzling storm, but they cannot hope to stand against the fury of the Doom Scythe's main weapon – the aptly named and rightly feared death ray.

There is seldom a warning before the death ray strikes, for any sound it makes is lost under the unearthly wailing of the Doom Scythe's engines. A particularly alert foe might recognise the nimbus of energy building up around the focussing crystal, or the abrupt change in air pressure, but few recognise the significance in time. The nimbus pulses one final time and an irresistible beam of blinding white light bursts from the Doom Scythe's underside, vaporising infantry and tanks alike, leaving only charred and rutted terrain in its wake. A single Doom Scythe can carve its way through an entire armoured column so long as its death ray remains operational, and a full squadron can reduce the sprawling spires of a hive city to fulminating slag in less than an hour.

	Type	BS	Armour		
			F	S	R
Doom Scythe	Fast, Skimmer	4	11	11	11

UNIT TYPE: Vehicle.

WARGEAR: Twin-linked tesla destructor.

Death ray: To fire the death ray, nominate a point on the battlefield anywhere within the weapon's range, then nominate a second point within 3D6" of the first. Then, draw a straight line between the two points. Every unit (friendly or enemy) underneath the line suffers a number of hits equal to the number of models in the unit underneath the line. If the vehicle's other weaponry is fired in the same shooting phase, it must be fired at one of the units hit by the death ray.

Range	Strength	AP	Type
12"(special)	10	1	Heavy 1

SPECIAL RULES: Deep Strike, Living Metal.

Aerial Assault: A Doom Scythe that moved at cruising speed can fire all of its weapons.

Supersonic: A Doom Scythe that moves flat out may move up to 36".

'Death comes in many forms, but I would count aerial bombardment amongst the most satisfyingly efficient.'
- *Executioner Ezandrakh of the Mephrit Dynasty*
Herald of the Red Harvest

NIGHT SCYTHES

The Night Scythe is the Necrons' favoured tool of invasion, a variant of the Doom Scythe that replaces some of the fighter's heaviest weaponry in favour of a troop transport capacity. This is not to say that the Night Scythe is in any way defenceless – quite the opposite. With its turret mounted tesla destructor, and the nerve-shredding shriek of its engines, the Night Scythe is still a formidable fighter craft in its own right.

Should a Phaeron wish to reach out his hand and reclaim one of the sundered planets, his first wave of attack inevitably includes a fleet of Night Scythes. Manoeuvrable enough to evade incoming fire from orbital defence platforms and swift enough to outpace mustering defenders, Night Scythes can ghost through a defence perimeter to deploy invasion forces directly at the heart of key enemy installations and strategic locations. Once a foot hold has been established, coordinates are relayed to the main army, enabling Monoliths and other forces to teleport into position, and the invasion to begin.

Unlike the armoured carriers employed by other races, the Night Scythe does not have a transport compartment as such. Instead, it deploys troops by means of a captive wormhole whose far end is anchored on a distant Tomb World. Though this is less flexible than the Monolith's eternity gate, it does allow the Night Scythe to mimic the battlefield role of a more conventional transport vehicle without jeopardising the existence of its assigned squad. If the Night Scythe is destroyed, its payload squad is simply isolated from the battle until an alternate means of deployment can be established. Though this invariably prevents the squad from taking part in the immediate battle, this is preferable to them being destroyed outright as they can join the campaign's later stages.

Night Scythes are often employed as far-ranging scout ships, tasked with making contact with other Tomb Worlds or searching out lost Necron planets suitable for reclamation. On worlds where the interlopers are either few in number or primitive in nature, the Night Scythe spearheads a ruthless subjugation. On worlds where other life forms have taken strong root, the pilot of the Night Scythe clandestinely performs probes and biopsies of the inhabitants, preying on isolated settlements or convoys whilst it searches for clues that will identify the inhabiting race's suitability for apotheosis. Such tests are long and exhaustive, and the pilot is often forced to dissect entire townships in order to harvest sufficient data. On a particularly promising planet, the Night Scythe's pilot may go so far as to transport living samples back to its Tomb World for further inspection by Crypteks. Most such subjects do not survive the scientific method, but are instead stripped down molecule by molecule and neuron by neuron. A few abductees are returned to their homes, but even these are implanted with mindshackle scarabs or other control mechanisms to enable them to function as unsuspecting spies and saboteurs who will pave the way for imminent invasion.

			Armour		
	Type	BS	F	S	R
Night Scythe	Fast, Skimmer	4	11	11	11

UNIT TYPE: Vehicle.

WARGEAR: Twin-linked tesla destructor.

TRANSPORT: The Night Scythe has a transport capacity of 15. It can carry jump infantry (each model takes up two points of transport capacity) and jetbikes (each model takes up three points of transport capacity). If the Night Scythe is destroyed, the embarked unit is not allowed to disembark, but instead enters reserve (when they arrive, they cannot Deep Strike).

Fire Points: None.

Access Points: Treat the wormhole gateway on the underside of the Night Scythe as its access point. For the purpose of embarking or disembarking from a Night Scythe, measure to and from the model's base. For example, models wishing to embark within a Night Scythe can do so if at the end of their movement, all models of the unit are within 2" of the Night Scythe base.

SPECIAL RULES: Deep Strike, Living Metal.

Aerial Assault: A Night Scythe that moved at cruising speed can fire all of its weapons.

Supersonic: A Night Scythe that moves flat out may move up to 36".

CATACOMB COMMAND BARGES

The more aggressive Necron Overlords fight not on foot, but rather from the deck of a Catacomb Command Barge – an armoured, repulsor-driven skimmer. In ancient times, this craft would hover high above the army, so that all Necrontyr could see their Overlord's presence and take heart from it. Most Overlords can no longer directly inspire the soldiery as once they could – few Necrons any longer have the capacity to process such emotions – but technology has filled the void. The Catacomb Command Barge is nothing less than a giant carrier wave generator that allows an Overlord to instantaneously issue commands to nearby troops. Even now, when inspiration has little to do with visibility, an Overlord will often seek a raised vantage point at battle's start, so he might better divine the enemy's intended strategy before it unfolds.

The Catacomb Command Barge itself is a swift and manoeuvrable craft – it has to be, for an Overlord must keep pace with the battle at all times. Though the Overlord is undeniably the Command Barge's master, he does not operate its controls. Such work is beneath nobility, and especially below those of such esteemed rank as he. Rather, the craft's controls are the charge of the two slaved Necron crew who act both as its pilots and as the gunners for its underslung weaponry. These Necrons are hard-wired to the Overlord through the craft and can react to his instructions in a fraction of a second. This does not, however, prevent the Overlord from issuing verbal commands – old habits die hard in old soldiers. Indeed, it is often possible to hear

the Overlord's authoritative instructions or angry epithets echoing across a battlefield as he drives his crew hard up to, and sometimes beyond, their limits. Service aboard a Command Barge is considered to be a great honour, though it is not without its risks. Not only does it guarantee a place in the very heart of battle, but if the Overlord is slain – or sometimes even if he is merely put to inconvenience through mechanical failure – retribution falls upon his pilots.

With his barge's systems attended to by his minions, the Overlord is free to wield his warscythe against the foe. Sometimes he will disembark before doing so, preferring to face his chosen foe with feet braced firmly on solid ground. At others, however, the Overlord will remain upon his Catacomb Command Barge, choosing instead to strike at the foe with great sweeps of his blade as his barge screams past. The last sight of many an enemy has been that of a Catacomb Command Barge swooping out of the sky with the Overlord's blade gleaming as it swings around in a decapitating arc...

	Type	BS	Armour		
			F	S	R
Catacomb Command Barge	Fast, Open-topped, Skimmer	4	11	11	11

UNIT TYPE: Vehicle.

TRANSPORT: The Catacomb Command Barge can carry one independent character.

WARGEAR: Quantum shielding, tesla cannon.

SPECIAL RULES: Living Metal.

Sweep Attack: Whilst a character remains embarked on a Catacomb Command Barge, he can make three special 'sweep' attacks each turn. These attacks can be made in the Movement phase against one enemy unit that the Catacomb Command Barge moves over. All attacks must be resolved on the same unit.

Roll To Hit and To Wound separately for each Sweep Attack. If the Catacomb Command Barge moved at combat speed this turn, a Sweep Attack hits on a 3+, otherwise it hits on a 4+. For each success, the unit suffers a hit at the character's Strength, plus any Strength bonuses and special abilities from his close combat weapon. Hits against vehicles are resolved against rear armour. On a Sweep Attack where the To Hit dice roll is a 6, you can choose which model the resulting Wound (if there is one) is allocated against. Cover saves are not permitted against Wounds caused by Sweep Attacks.

Symbiotic Repair: If the Catacomb Command Barge suffers an immobilised or weapon destroyed result, the embarked character can reduce his remaining Wounds by 1 to negate the result. This cannot be done if it would cause the character to be removed as a casualty.

GHOST ARKS

There have been Ghost Arks since the very earliest days of the Necrontyr. Then, they were simple wooden carriages pulled by toiling beasts of burden, commissioned by families of the dead to convey corpses from their homes to their place of interment. Thousands of years later, at the time of biotransference, the now-motorised Ghost Arks took on darker connotations. Guided by grim-faced soldiers, they prowled the streets of the great cities. No longer was their business with the dead, but with the living, for they were the means by which unwilling citizens were dragged to the great transformative machines.

Though the leaders of the Necrontyr had pledged their allegiance to the C'tan, few of the common people wished for the change that was upon them. So did the Ghost Arks often convey the broken bodies of those beaten near unto death by the government's enforcers, for only a spark of life and memory was required for biotransference. As resistance grew, the Ghost Arks were crewed no longer by soldiers of flesh and blood, but by the first wave of converted Necrons; and with that, all pretence at mercy and compassion ended. With each load of living cargo the Ghost Arks claimed, their reputation grew ever darker and their aspect ever more bleak. By the time biotransference was almost complete, the mere sight of a Ghost Ark was enough to provoke terror in those observers who could any longer feel such things. Those still living who saw the Ghost Arks about their work swore that the tortured souls of their victims flew thick about the wagons, haunting the air with mournful voices.

Much has changed for the Necrons in the countless millennia since, and the role of the Ghost Ark has changed with it. No longer the gaolers of the living, they are now the redeemers of the fallen, tasked with trawling the battlefields for remnants of Necrons no longer able to reconstruct themselves. Recovered components are then set upon by swarms of constructor scarabs. Working with near-silent efficiency, they return the fallen Necron to function if repairs are possible, or dissolve it into reusable raw energy if they are not. Repaired Necrons are then locked in stasis until the Ghost Ark is at capacity, at which point it will either return its salvaged cargo to their Tomb World or else deploy them directly to the battlefield.

Ghost Arks are often pressed into service as conventional transport vehicles, conveying reinforcements to some vital area of the battlefield, or allowing Necron forces to attack from an unexpected quarter. The enemy's predicament is made all the worse by the fact that Necrons deployed in this fashion are, to all intents and purposes, accompanied by their own mobile repair station. Only by destroying the Ghost Ark can the foe have any hope of victory.

	Type	BS	Armour F	S	R
Ghost Ark	Open-topped, Skimmer	4	11	11	11

UNIT TYPE: Vehicle.

WARGEAR: Quantum shielding.

Two gauss flayer arrays: The Ghost Ark has two separate arrays of five gauss flayers – one along each flank – enabling it to 'broadside' enemy units. The two arrays can shoot at different targets, although all guns in the same array must shoot at the same target.

TRANSPORT: The Ghost Ark has a transport capacity of ten models. It can only carry Necron Warriors, Necron Lords, Overlords, Crypteks and the Necron special characters.

SPECIAL RULES: Living Metal.

Repair Barge: At the start of each Necron Movement phase, a Ghost Ark can expend energy to repair fallen Necrons. Nominate a unit of Necron Warriors within 6" (or embarked on) the Ghost Ark and roll a D6. If the score is a 2 or more, add D3 models to the unit – the models can move and act normally this turn. This cannot take the unit beyond its starting size. If a model cannot be placed for any reason, it is destroyed. On a roll of a 1, place the models as described above, however the Ghost Ark is drained and suffers a glancing hit with no saves allowed.

'Immortality is not quite the same as invulnerability, but it is close enough.'

- Illuminor Szeras
Cryptek Overseer of the Zantragora Conclave

IMOTEKH THE STORMLORD
Phaeron of the Sautekh Dynasty

Nemesor Imotekh awoke from the Great Sleep to find his Tomb World in disarray. Mandragora had survived the aeons mostly intact, only to fall foul of unrestrained ambition. The crownworld's Phaeron had been one of the few to perish during hibernation and, once they had quashed immediate alien threats, the remaining nobles had moved to seize the throne. A decade of internecine civil war followed, with no faction able to gain victory. During this time, the revivification of high-ranking nobles was suspended, as neither side wished to awaken further competitors. Had the situation continued, Imotekh would likely have slumbered until the civil war had torn Mandragora apart. As it was, one of the pretenders struck upon the idea of recruiting the famous general to his cause – with such a supporter in thrall, victory could not fail to be his.

However, when Imotekh awoke, he was both enraged and appalled at the anarchy about him. Realising that Mandragora's only hope of restoration lay in the civil war ending as swiftly as possible, he refused to support either faction. Instead, Imotekh marshalled an army of his own, destroyed the chief antagonists, and claimed Mandragora's throne for himself. The newly crowned Phaeron thereafter forbade any form of infighting within his realm, declaring such activities to be a waste of time, effort and resource. This law was ill-observed at first, but swiftly became the norm once

Imotekh had proven his willingness to make terminal examples of those who flouted his authority. Between this rule of iron and a swift string of military successes against nearby worlds, Imotekh's position soon became unassailable. Indeed, to this day his only true rival is the famed Nemesor Zahndrekh of the crownworld of Gidrim, but the old general's loyalty is as unquestionable as his wits are addled, so he is of little threat.

Imotekh is a grand strategist, perhaps the most accomplished the galaxy has ever known. His campaigns operate not only across worlds, but across entire star systems and sectors. When Imotekh launches an attack, it is impossible to discern if it is the main thrust of his strategy or simply a decoy raid, crafted to bleed enemy reinforcements away from a battle yet to come. All such assaults are carefully weighted to overwhelm enemy forces already in place, requiring the foe to either sacrifice his troops or reinforce them – and Imotekh's plans are always many stages ahead, set to take advantage of either course. Indeed, the Stormlord's battle plans are incredibly versatile, seeded with feint attacks, counter-strategies and other contingencies enacted automatically should certain circumstances be triggered or thresholds crossed. To outside observers there is something almost mystical to Imotekh's methodology, for how else could he so flawlessly anticipate the unseen? Yet in truth there is nothing more at play here than the careful application of probabilities and logic, combined with a canny understanding of the foe's mindset.

So impeccable are the logical patterns behind the Stormlord's strategies that the only way a foe can truly gain meaningful advantage is to abandon all logic themselves – something that most enemies find incredibly difficult to do, but Orkish anarchy achieves as naturally as breathing. Thus does the Stormlord hate Orks above all the lesser races of the galaxy for, no matter how hard he tries, he rarely wins a lasting victory over the rabblesome greenskins. Yet lasting victories against the Orks there must be, for Imotekh's goal is nothing less than to wipe them from the face of the galaxy. The Stormlord is unshakeable in his belief that only when the galaxy is washed clean with the blood of inferior beings will Necron dominance begin anew.

As Phaeron of the Sautekh Dynasty, Imotekh can draw upon incredible resources, for the armies of the entire dynasty are his to requisition at need. Yet the Stormlord knows that the foe – all other sentient life – is too numerous for victory to be won through force of arms alone. Thus, for Imotekh, terror is a weapon as potent as any in the Necron arsenal, and one he employs to full effect. His armies advance under the cover of storm-blackened skies, emerald lightning bolts arcing out from heavy clouds to wreak carnage amongst the foe. Enemy armies that advance into the shadow of the storm are simply swallowed up, cut off from all contact whilst the battle lasts. Any warriors that escape from the maelstrom's clutches do so only to sow panic, fear and dismay amongst their comrades. Worse, some such survivors are implanted with bloodswarm nanoscarabs, whose gore-warm scent acts as an irresistible beacon for roaming packs of Flayed Ones.

If the Stormlord has one weakness, it is a prideful need to display his superiority over those enemy commanders foolish enough to stand against him. High ranking enemies are often set free upon their defeat so that they will have to live with the knowledge of their inadequacy. This is a lesson invariably reinforced by physical mutilation – a severed limb normally being the favoured method. Yet with every battle, these surviving foes learn a little more of the Stormlord's methods and the best of them only become more determined to see his campaigns ended once and for all. High Marshal Helbrecht of the Black Templars, in particular, has run the Stormlord close on more than one occasion, though victory has thus far escaped his grasp.

The fact that Imotekh suffers from such a personal form of martial hubris stands in stark contrast to the analytical and emotionless detachment he displays when planning and conducting campaigns. It is possible that stasis-induced eccentricity is to blame, but for which trait? Is Imotekh a master strategist whose engrammic damage spurs him to seek personal glory, or a bellicose warrior granted strategic genius through an accident of fate? In the end, it does not matter. If Imotekh's defeat comes, it is sure not to be at the hands of a superior strategist, but rather at the hands of a more accomplished warrior.

And there will be many opportunities for such a downfall. Imotekh's domain is growing at a rate unparalleled amongst the Necron dynasties. Four score Tomb Worlds lie under his regal command, and five times as many alien-held planets pay direct or indirect tribute – the number of alien civilisations Imotekh has destroyed during his campaigns cannot easily be counted. Such a realm is as nothing when compared to the galaxy-spanning Imperium or the Necron dynasties at the height of their glory, but is nonetheless impressive for the work of a mere two hundred years.

Such expansion has come at a price, however, and Imotekh's dynasty is now starting to come to the notice of several other realms. On Macragge, reports of Necron activity beyond Ultramar's northern borders have reached the attention of Marneus Calgar. Iyanden's Farseers have sensed a peril before their craftworld that is, in its way, as great a threat as the Tyranid menace that lies behind. Rumours of a sinister power on the march have reached even the Tau Empire though, as ever, their prevailing interpretation is one of opportunity, rather than threat. It is only a matter of time before the Sautekh Dynasty comes into direct conflict with these other realms, and if forced to war with two or more at the same time, Imotekh's genius will surely be tested.

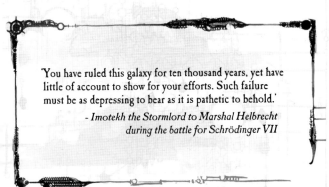

'You have ruled this galaxy for ten thousand years, yet have little of account to show for your efforts. Such failure must be as depressing to bear as it is pathetic to behold.'
- Imotekh the Stormlord to Marshal Helbrecht during the battle for Schrödinger VII

	WS	BS	S	T	W	I	A	Ld	Sv
Imotekh the Stormlord	4	4	5	5	3	2	3	10	2+

UNIT TYPE: Infantry (Character).

WARGEAR: Gauntlet of fire, phase shifter, phylactery, sempiternal weave.

Bloodswarm nanoscarabs: At the start of the first game turn, randomly choose one non-vehicle unit in the enemy army. This unit is infested with bloodswarm nanoscarabs – any Flayed One packs entering play via Deep Strike do not scatter if they aim to arrive within 6" of this unit.

Staff of the Destroyer: This ancient and ornamental staff of light was first wielded by Zehet, founder of the Sautekh Dynasty, and has seen battle in the hands of every one of his successors. The staff can unleash a searing beam of unbelievably destructive pan-dimensional energy. Once triggered, the Staff of the Destroyer takes some time to rebuild its charge.

Range	Strength	AP	Type
*2D6"	6	1	Assault 1, One use only

*When firing the Staff of the Destroyer, nominate a direction. Then roll 2D6 and extend a straight line from Imotekh's base in the chosen direction, a distance equal to the total rolled. Any unit, friendly or enemy, under this line takes a number of hits equal to the number of models in the unit under the line.

SPECIAL RULES: Ever-living, Independent Character, Phaeron (see page 30), Reanimation Protocols.

Humiliating Defeat: If a Character loses its final Wound to Imotekh's close combat attacks, roll a D3. Imotekh counts as having scored this many extra wounds for the purposes of calculating the assault result.

Hyperlogical Strategy: An army that includes Imotekh the Stormlord seizes the initiative on a roll of 4+. However, greenskins always manage to confound his plans somehow, so an army that includes Imotekh can never attempt to seize the initiative against Orks.

Lord of the Storm: If your army includes Imotekh the Stormlord, the Night Fighting rules automatically apply during the first game turn. Furthermore, you can attempt to keep the Night Fighting rules in play in subsequent game turns by rolling a D6 at the start of the turn. If the result is greater than the turn number, the storm continues and the Night Fighting rules remain in play. If not, the Night Fighting rules cease to be in effect and are not used for the rest of the battle.

In addition, whilst the Night Fighting rules remain in play, roll a D6 for each unengaged enemy unit on the battlefield at the start of each Necron Shooting phase. On a roll of a 6, that unit is struck by a bolt of lightning and suffers D6 Strength 8, AP 5 hits (vehicles are hit on their side armour). Note that Night Fighting rules brought into play by a Solar Pulse (see page 84) do not generate lightning.

ILLUMINOR SZERAS

The C'tan might have provided the knowledge for biotransference, but it was Szeras who made it a reality. Even then, he saw it as the first of several steps on the path to ultimate evolution, a journey that would end as a creature not of flesh or metal, but as a god of pure energy. Until that day, Szeras is driven to take full advantage of his android form. After all, no longer must he sleep nor deal with the thousand frailties and distractions to which flesh is heir.

Szeras labours to unravel the mysteries of life, for he fears that he would be a poor sort of god without the secrets of life at his fingertips. Szeras has been on the brink of understanding for many centuries, yet somehow final comprehension always escapes him. Perhaps there are some concepts in the universe that do not reveal themselves before logic, or perhaps it is simply that to understand life, the observer must stand amongst the ranks of the living, and not the undead. Whatever the reason, the truth is that the secrets of the soul will almost certainly lie forever beyond Szeras' comprehension. This is a truth that he will never accept. Yet, at times, Szeras must turn aside from his work and act in the interest of others – he requires a constant flow of living subjects, and the most efficient way for him to acquire such creatures is to trade expertise in exchange for captives.

Though Szeras is obsessed with the secrets of life, his aptitude for augmenting the weaponry, and even the mechanical bodies of his fellow Necrons is peerless. Szeras'

delving into the form and function of so many disparate living creatures has taught him how to augment almost every facet of Necron machinery – a trait seen as distasteful by many of his peers. The dissection of Vuzsalen Arachtoid compound eyes unlocked an improved array for targeting optics, and the molecular dissembling of chitinous Ambull hide led the way to more efficient armour configurations, to name but two of many thousands of such advances.

On occasion, Szeras' talents are in such demand that he can name his own price – invariably a harvesting raid targeted against a world of his choosing. Above all, Szeras cherishes Eldar subjects, as they inevitably produce more intriguing results than any other of the galaxy's creatures. However, few Necron Overlords will deliberately transgress on Eldar territory for reasons other than solid military gain, so Szeras finds such specimens the hardest of all to acquire. Szeras inevitably accompanies the initial waves of such an attack, the better to pick and choose the subjects that will make up his payment and ensure he is not cheated by his client.

Once seized, Szeras' specimens can look forward only to a pain-filled, though not necessarily brief, existence in the bloodstained and shadowed laboratory catacombs of Zantragora. Few of Szeras' operations are carried out on the dead, for he believes the knowledge he seeks resides only in the living. Banks of stasis machinery keep the subject alive and aware throughout the procedures, though they do nothing to numb the terrible pain. The specimens' agonised screams are of no consequence to Szeras as he feels no kinship with such inferior beings. He simply shuts off his audio receptors until the repulsive noise subsides, watching impassively as his whirring tools carve the subject apart molecule by molecule.

	WS	BS	S	T	W	I	A	Ld	Sv
Illuminor Szeras	4	4	4	4	2	2	4	10	3+

UNIT TYPE: Infantry (Character).

WARGEAR: Eldritch lance (see page 84), gaze of flame (see page 84).

SPECIAL RULES: Ever-living, Independent Character, Reanimation Protocols.

Mechanical Augmentation: At the start of the game, before forces have been deployed, nominate one unit of Necron Warriors or Immortals to be the recipient of Szeras' upgrades. That unit receives one upgrade from the following list – roll a D6 to determine which:

1-2 Hardened Carapace: The unit is Toughness 5 for the duration of the game.

3-4 Improved Optics: The unit is Ballistic Skill 5 for the duration of the game.

5-6 Enhanced Servomotors: The unit is Strength 5 for the duration of the game.

ORIKAN THE DIVINER

Orikan is a consummate astromancer, able to calculate the events of the future from the patterns of the stars. Thus did he know of the Fall of the Eldar, the Rise of Man, the Horus Heresy and the coming of the Tyranids many thousands of years before they came to pass. Through careful study and scrutiny, Orikan can even divine lesser occurrences: the movement of fleets, the destinies of individuals, even the strategies undertaken by campaigning armies – events not important enough to reshape the galaxy, but the foreknowledge of which can dramatically change the fortunes of the beholder.

Though they make use of his laborious studies, few amongst Orikan's peers truly trust him. This is not altogether to do with his skills, for all Crypteks are capable of techno-sorceries that defy belief. The unease that Orikan provokes is due chiefly to the mocking scorn with which he treats the nobility of every rank, and to the knowing gleam in his eye that implies he is party to a joke that no other can perceive. Many an Overlord would dearly like to see Orikan punished for this quiet insolence. However, not only is such a course of action impolitic – the benefits of being able to call upon Orikan's skills greatly outweigh any offence caused by his manner – it is also almost entirely impossible. Orikan knows the plans of his rivals and enemies long before they do, and it is child's play for him to exploit such schemes to his personal advantage – an alteration that, more often than not, involves a fatal outcome for the original plotter.

Skilled astromancer though he is, Orikan's predictions are not flawless. Unforeseen events can queer his calculations, wiping out and replacing his prophesied timeline. Warp travel is a consistent aggravation, as its eddies and anarchies seem to delight in defying his predictions. Under such circumstances, to preserve his plans and reputation, Orikan is forced to employ a closely guarded set of chronomantic abilities. Travelling backwards down his own timeline, he emerges in the past at a point at which he can set his prophesied version of the future back on track, normally by having the interfering factor destroyed in some manner.

In Orikan's predictions, the Imperial Navy dockyards on Helios VI should never have survived the onset of Waaagh! Skullkrak, and did so only by an inconvenient intervention by the meddlesome Silver Skulls 4th Company. By retroactively arranging for the Space Marines to be ambushed and nearly wiped out by Necron forces some weeks earlier, Orikan ensured that the destruction of Helios VI ultimately occurred as first foreseen. Thus were the Necrons able to reclaim much of the surrounding sector but, more importantly, thus was Orikan's reputation kept intact.

Yet Orikan has ever been sparing of such actions, for his meddling can birth all manner of unforeseen events. As a direct result of the Helios VI affair, no less than five Space Marine Chapters, including the Death Spectres, Howling Griffons and the remainder of the Silver Skulls, descended upon the Lazar system to take revenge, utterly destroying the Tomb World from whence Orikan's original commission had come. In that case, Orikan's culpability in the disaster remained secret, but it could have easily gone otherwise.

Orikan takes great care to keep his machinations hidden from his peers. Though chronomancy is a science practiced by many other Crypteks, no other is remotely capable of Orikan's feats, something that would increase a hundredfold the suspicion in which he is held. And suspicion is the last thing Orikan needs at this moment. A thousand millennia of planning and preparation are about to come to fruition, once the stars are in the proper alignment, Orikan will finally embrace his true destiny...

	WS	BS	S	T	W	I	A	Ld	Sv
Orikan	4	4	4	4	2	2	2	10	4+
*Orikan Empowered	5	5	7	7	4	4	4	10	4+

UNIT TYPE: Infantry (Character).

WARGEAR: Phase shifter, transdimensional beamer.

Staff of Tomorrow: Orikan's staff exists a half second ahead of 'now', his blows hitting the target an instant before he moves to strike.

Orikan re-rolls failed To Hit rolls in close combat. Wounds caused by the Staff of Tomorrow ignore armour saves.

SPECIAL RULES: Ever-living, Independent Character, Reanimation Protocols.

Lord of Time: This ability can be used once, at the start of one of your turns. For the remainder of that turn, any unsuccessful reserve rolls must be re-rolled.

*The Stars Are Right: Orikan starts the game with the first of the two profiles given above but, as the game progresses, there is a chance that the stars will come into alignment and restore to him a portion of ancient power. Roll a D6 at the start of each of your turns. If the dice roll is less than or equal to the turn number, then the constellations have come into alignment and Orikan has unlocked a portion of celestial power (bwahahaha!). Orikan henceforth uses the 'Orikan Empowered' profile (it's still the same model). Once Orikan powers up, continue to roll a D6 at the start of each of your turns; if the result is less than or equal to the turn number, the power recedes, Orikan returns to his initial profile and no further transformation rolls are made. Wounds suffered are carried over between incarnations (which can mean that Orikan is removed as a casualty if he transforms back to his weaker incarnation).

Temporal Snares: During the first game turn, all enemy units that move count as moving through difficult terrain. If they are actually moving through difficult terrain, then a unit can move the lowest D6 result of their difficult terrain test, rather than the highest.

> 'Time is a weapon like any other. If nothing else, I can simply wait for my foes to rot.'
>
> – Orikan the Diviner

TRAZYN THE INFINITE
Archeovist of the Solemnace Galleries

Trazyn is a preserver of histories, artefacts and events. The vast and numberless vaults burrowed through the Tomb World of Solemnace are crowded with technologies so rare and sublime that any Adeptus Mechanicus Tech-Priest would give the life of several close colleagues just to know that they existed. The sunken chambers are crowded with artefacts of all forms: the fabled wraithbone choir of Altansar, the preserved head of Sebastian Thor, the ossified husk of an Enslaver and a giant of a man clad in baroque power armour, his face contorted in a permanent scream – to name but a few. It is a hoard ever growing, for history is always on the march, and Trazyn strives to keep pace. Alas, few worlds willingly give the artefacts Trazyn seeks of them, selfishly clutching onto the few meaningful things in their civilisation, rather than offering them up to be preserved through the ages. In such circumstances, Trazyn has little choice but to muster his armies and take them by force – if this results in the destruction of a city, a planet or an entire sector, so be it.

Most impressive of all Solemnace's wonders are the prismatic galleries, winding chambers of statuary recapturing events from history that Trazyn deems worthy of preservation, ranging in scale from the last high council of Idharae Craftworld, to the sprawling massacres on Tragus. The prismatic galleries are populated not with mere sculpture, but living beings transmuted into hard-light holograms by arcane technology. Some such statues are nothing less than the original enactors of history, frozen in the moment of triumph or defeat and whisked away to Solemnace to forever stand as testament to their deeds. Occasionally a statue will be destroyed, shattered by a malfunctioning Canoptek Wraith's collision, the collapse of a gallery's ceiling or, as happened on one catastrophic occasion, a firefight between Trazyn's warrior-servants and the entourage of an all-too-curious Inquisitor (most of whom now constitute their own display in one of the upper galleries). Such events drive Trazyn to frustration, for he must halt his search for fresh acquisitions and seek out replacements.

Of course, few of the statues are replaceable, but there are no rules to Trazyn's galleries save those that he himself decides upon. If he decides one of the hard-light tableaus fulfils its function with substitutes – however inaccurate – then he will acquire them. Fully one tenth of his 'Death of Lord Solar Macharius' gallery is populated by holographic Imperial Guardsmen whose uniforms are three hundred years astray from historical fact, but Trazyn cares only for the spectacle, not the details of bootlaces and buttonholes. Once Trazyn has resolved to refresh his galleries, he does so with great urgency, seeking out campaigning armies, vulnerable garrisons or populated worlds with flawed planetary defences. Depending on the scale of losses, replenishment might be achieved by a few simple kidnappings by low-flying Night Scythes, or may need a more substantial mobilisation to process and catalogue portions of planetary population.

Nor are Tomb Worlds immune to Trazyn's attentions. In his mind, other Necrons are no more trustworthy than aliens when it comes to guardianship of the artefacts he craves. Thus Trazyn makes little distinction between artefacts held on alien worlds and those possessed by his own kind. The resulting indiscrete 'liberations' have rendered him persona non grata on several Tomb Worlds. He is forbidden entirely from the catacombs of Mandragora under pain of death, following a long-ago attempt to spirit away the Staff of the Destroyer, and welcomed on Moebius on the strict understanding that his arrival will in some way improve the standing of the ruling Nekthyst Dynasty.

These occurrences go some way to explain why Trazyn rarely travels under his own name, but with his true identity concealed by pseudonym. Alas, whilst he fancies these names to be masterful attempts at deception, all are simply plucked from ancient Necron myth or fabled literature, such as Nemesor Koschai or Thantekh the Deathless. That Trazyn is rarely discovered before he is ready to make his move, therefore, says rather more about the insular nature and selective knowledge of other Necron nobles than it does his own aptitude for subterfuge. Even on Ork-held planets, Tau Sept worlds and human colonies, where his dealings are conducted strictly through mindshackled cat's-paws, Trazyn goes to great pains to keep his identity a secret. He knows full well that his activities have come to the attention of certain Rogue Traders and Inquisitors – after all, the Imperium's

tangled history presents something of an irresistible lure to one such as Trazyn. Nonetheless, while he remains confident in his ability to outwit the plots and snares of primitive humans, Trazyn's paranoia is sufficient to force a degree of caution.

Trazyn commonly conducts reconnaissance and campaigns through surrogates – substitute bodies into which he can pour his will. Should the body suffer catastrophic damage, Trazyn's essence simply returns to his 'true' form, or otherwise into another surrogate.

Not all Trazyn's substitutes are immediately recognisable as such. Indeed many surrogates are actually Necrons Lords or Overlords in their own right who, unbeknownst to them, have had their bodies subverted by Trazyn. Should he need to occupy such a body, he can do so as easily as he could any other surrogate – the regular occupant's will is suppressed for the duration of Trazyn's occupation, and the body itself instantly morphs into an exact facsimile of his primary form. Thus protected from the dangers of a perilous galaxy, Trazyn can go wherever his passion for preservation takes him.

Yet these days of caution and plotting are fast passing by. The raucous din of war grows louder in every corner of the galaxy, consuming temples, cities, worlds and even entire races long before Trazyn has had the opportunity to catalogue and 'rescue' all that is worth saving. Thus, for the first time in millions of years, Trazyn is mobilising the full might of Solemnace's legions – the better to secure entire planets from the onset of ignorant barbarians whilst a proper and detailed cultural survey is undertaken. Already a score of the Imperium's worlds are under occupation by Trazyn's forces, the inhabitants subjugated by his implacable minions, but the legions of Solemnace show no signs of stopping.

	WS	BS	S	T	W	I	A	Ld	Sv
Trazyn the Infinite	4	4	5	5	3	2	3	10	3+

UNIT TYPE: Infantry (Character).

WARGEAR: Mindshackle Scarabs.

Empathic Obliterator: The exact provenance of this peculiar stave remains unknown to everyone but Trazyn, but it is rumoured to contain technology designed by the long-vanished Old Ones. Should the Empathic Obliterator slay an enemy, a psionic shockwave ripples out from the body of the victim, striking down all nearby creatures of similar mind and purpose. It is therefore an ideal weapon for a being such as Trazyn, who disdains exhaustive physical combat and far prefers a single telling blow at the opportune moment.

If Trazyn kills one or more enemies in close combat, the Empathic Obliterator unleashes a psionic shockwave. This occurs after all blows have been struck, but before the Assault Results are determined.

To resolve the psionic shockwave, roll a D6 for every model in the combat (friendly and enemy) with exactly the same name on their characteristic profile as a model slain by Trazyn that phase. If the score is 4 or more, that model suffers a Wound (armour saves are taken as normal). For example, if Trazyn

slew a Space Marine Sergeant, roll for all other Space Marine Sergeants in the combat; if Trazyn slew an Ork Boy, roll for all other Ork Boyz in the combat.

Wounds caused by the psionic shockwave count towards the Assault Result.

SPECIAL RULES: Ever-living, Independent Character, Phaeron (see page 30), Reanimation Protocols.

'Excellent! Another Piece for the Collection': Trazyn is a scoring unit and can claim objectives. He's not really capturing a martial objective, as such, but is seeking to claim an artefact hidden nearby – any military gains as a result of this are totally coincidental (but no less useful for Trazyn's controlling player).

Surrogate Hosts: If Trazyn is removed from play as a casualty, roll a D6. On a score of 1, remove Trazyn from play as normal. If the score is 2 or more, randomly choose another model from all the friendly Lychguards, Crypteks, Necron Lords and Overlords on the table (not counting special character versions of any of the above). Remove the nominated model from play as a casualty, and return Trazyn to play in its place – his remaining Wounds are now equal to the number of Wounds the removed model had remaining. Trazyn only awards kill points once he has been slain and does not return. Models removed because they have been replaced by Trazyn award kill points as normal.

'Dear lady, let me express my fulsome appreciation for your most generous gift. It is so very rare to discover another of my own kind that appreciates my work, therefore to find understanding amongst a member of another race is nothing short of a revelation.

I realise that you briefly trod my galleries, but the fact that you spotted in so short a time that my Acabrius War collection was lacking three regiments of Catachan warriors reveals that you truly have a collector's eye for detail. And to send five regiments! Such generosity will allow me to weed out and replace a few of the more substandard pieces in my collection.

If I might level a minor criticism, the instructions issued to your gift were manifestly not as clear as you thought, as most of them had to be forcibly restrained – sadly it seems that the lower orders will always behave like an army of invasion, whether that be their purpose or not. However, this is a minor complaint and seems almost churlish under the circumstances, so please allow me to repay your gift with one of my own. Accompanying this message is the Hyperstone Maze, one of a series of tesseract labyrinths constructed at the height of the Charnovokh Dynasty. It is a trinket really, of interest only to scholars such as you and I, but I trust you will find it amusing – assuming you have the wit to escape its clutches, of course.'

– hyperscroll message from Trazyn the Infinite to Inquisitor Valeria, c887.805.M41

The Army of Aeons Past

NEMESOR ZAHNDREKH & VARGARD OBYRON

Nemesor Zahndrekh was once counted amongst the greatest generals in the dynasties. By his campaigns of conquest did the world of Gidrim rise from ruling a small and insignificant planet on the fringes of the galaxy, to the iron-handed governance of a dozen star systems. Even now, though Gidrim has been subsumed into the Sautekh Dynasty, Zahndrekh is numbered amongst the mightiest of heroes. It is a reputation well deserved, for Gidrim is one of the more expansionist of the recently awoken crownworlds, and Zahndrekh's armies are an ever-present peril upon the galaxy's eastern fringe.

Yet for all his military genius, Zahndrekh does not see reality as it truly is. His mind suffered damage during the Great Sleep, and as a consequence he is trapped deep in the past, in the Wars of Secession that wracked his corner of the dynasties. In his mind, he fights these campaigns still as a creature of flesh and blood, crushing rebellious kings and bringing their domains back into the fold. He does not see armies of Orks, Eldar or Men, but hosts of rebellious kinsmen battling to sunder his beloved dynasties. As such, Zahndrekh is one of the few Necron Overlords to employ the full protocols of honourable war against all encroachers – where others see aliens, he sees only Necrontyr. He disdains the use of Deathmarks, assassin Wraiths and other strategies forbidden by the codes of battle – not that his subordinates

have any such compunction. Wherever possible, Zahndrekh ensures that enemy commanders are captured, not killed, and thereafter treated as honoured prisoners – much to the outraged consternation of Zahndrekh's Royal Court.

Indeed, there are many Lords in Zahndrekh's Royal Court who would dearly love to see the old general removed from power, for they judge that his adrift perceptions greatly outweigh his feats of battle. However, as befits his station, Zahndrekh has formidable defences against regicide. His personal sepulchre is heavily woven with traps, his personal household retinue boasts three entire legions of Lychguard, and he even employs four-score food tasters – even though it has been countless millennia since any morsel passed his lips. Yet Zahndrekh has one defence greater than all others – his aide and protector, Vargard Obyron.

Obyron served as Zahndrekh's vargard in their very first campaign – an undignified but hugely successful series of skirmishes in the swamps of Yama – and has stood steadfast at his side ever since, both on the field of battle and off it. Unlike his master, Obyron is very much aware of the changes wrought upon their existence, but has long since abandoned any attempt to awaken Zahndrekh to reality – whatever the fault in his master's mind, the damage lies too deep. So, like any dedicated servant, Obyron attends to all the loose ends created by Zahndrekh's eccentricities, chief of which are seeing to it that 'honoured' prisoners of war are 'killed whilst trying to escape', and that upstart Lords of the Royal Court are either silenced or disposed of.

Obyron's instincts for Gidrim's politics are every bit as finely tuned as Zahndrekh's are for battle. It is quite impossible for any plot to mature without word of it reaching Obyron, at which point he takes action to ensure it dies. The exact method depends greatly on what Obyron considers to have the greatest impact. A public trial by combat for the chief plotter is invariably Obyron's favoured method – his skill with a blade, legendary long before biotransference, has decayed little with the passing millennia. Sometimes however, Obyron deems the quiet terror of a conspirator's disappearance to have a more enduring effect. Regardless of method, Obyron has proven his supremacy hundreds of times over, yet every few decades, another upstart noble foolishly chances his arm against the Overlord of Gidrim who, for his part, is content to leave the vargard to his work. On many other worlds, Necron or otherwise, Obyron would be considered the true power behind the throne, yet his loyalty to Zahndrekh is total and completely without guile. He seeks no reward beyond continued service, and has never displayed an iota of desire to rule through his master.

On campaign, Zahndrekh and Obyron have proven to be an almost undefeatable combination. Zahndrekh seldom lowers himself to personal combat, but instead wields as a weapon the battlefield acumen that somehow remains undimmed by his faltering memory. Under his gaze, the Necron armies of Gidrim react almost instantaneously to counter enemy strategies, shifting between aggressive and defensive postures at a moment's notice. With a few carefully chosen words of

command, outflanking foes are isolated and crushed, enemy assault waves dispersed, and fire support positions obliterated. Such is Zahndrekh's crystal-perfect reading of the flow of battle that even the enemy's experienced veterans often seem like raw and fumbling recruits as their every tactic is anticipated and their every skill countered. For his part, Obyron fights in the front lines, wielding his warscythe with a precision to be expected of a warrior who counts his campaigns by the thousand. Yet no matter how distant he is, Obyron always keeps close watch on Zahndrekh – his responsibilities as bodyguard outweigh any other considerations. Should Zahndrekh be threatened, Obyron always returns to his master's side.

It is well that Obyron is so dedicated, for few Lords of Gidrim are eager to fight alongside their nemesor. Some simply cannot tolerate Zahndrekh's constant stream of reminiscences to battles fought long ago, relevant to the campaign at hand though those recollections always are. For others, Zahndrekh's damaged mind is a constant reminder of the fate that might one day be theirs, should need dictate they enter stasis-sleep once more. None of them see that such damage has doubtless already been wrought – that they are, in truth, just as blind to their own involuntarily idiosyncrasies as Zahndrekh is to his own.

NEMESOR ZAHNDREKH

	WS	BS	S	T	W	I	A	Ld	Sv
Nemesor Zahndrekh	4	4	5	5	3	2	3	10	2+

UNIT TYPE: Infantry (Character).

WARGEAR: Phase shifter, resurrection orb, sempiternal weave, staff of light.

SPECIAL RULES: Ever-living, Independent Character, Reanimation Protocols.

Adaptive Tactics: At the start of each of your turns in which Zahndrekh is on the battlefield, choose one friendly unit, then choose one of the following special rules: Counter-attack, Furious Charge, Hit and Run, Night Vision/Acute Senses, Stealth and Tank Hunters. The chosen unit has the chosen special rule until the start of your next turn.

Counter Tactics: At the start of each of your turns in which Zahndrekh is on the battlefield, choose one enemy unit within his line of sight. That unit loses the following special rules (if it has them), and cannot gain them, until the start of your next turn: Acute Senses, Counter-attack, Furious Charge, Hit and Run, Night Vision, Stealth and Tank Hunters.

Phased Reinforcements: If Zahndrekh is on the battlefield, any number of units in reserve that are able to Deep Strike can choose to enter play in the enemy turn, via Deep Strike, immediately after any enemy unit has arrived from reserve, normally during the enemy's Movement phase.

VARGARD OBYRON

	WS	BS	S	T	W	I	A	Ld	Sv
Vargard Obyron	6	4	5	5	3	2	3	10	2+

UNIT TYPE: Infantry (Character).

WARGEAR: Sempiternal weave, warscythe.

Ghostwalk Mantle: Obyron commissioned this advanced design Veil of Darkness from Gidrim's most accomplished psychomancer, Dagon of the Shadowed Matrix. It can spirit Obyron across the battlefield at a command, allowing him to stand at Zahndrekh's side whenever there is need.

Obyron can use the Ghostwalk Mantle in his Movement phase instead of moving normally. If he does, Obyron and his unit are removed from the tabletop and replaced together anywhere on the board using the rules for Deep Strike. Unlike other veils of darkness, the Ghostwalk Mantle can even be used if Obyron or his unit are locked in combat. Any enemy units no longer locked in combat as a result of this move consolidate immediately.

SPECIAL RULES: Ever-living, Independent Character, Reanimation Protocols.

Cleaving Counterblow: When enemies attempt to strike Obyron in close combat, keep track of the number of Attacks that fail To Hit (misses that are successfully re-rolled do not count towards this total) before Obyron makes his own attacks. For each miss, Obyron makes a bonus Attack (up to a maximum of 6 bonus Attacks) when it is his turn to strike. Enemy misses that occur after Obyron has attacked do not generate bonus Attacks. Any bonus Attacks not used by the end of the Assault phase are lost.

The Vargard's Duty: If Obyron uses his Ghostwalk Mantle, he does not scatter providing that he aims to arrive within 6" of Zahndrekh. Furthermore, if an enemy unit launches an assault on Zahndrekh's unit, Obyron immediately leaves his unit and must pile in to that combat, regardless of how far from it he is – we assume he uses the Ghostwalk Mantle to reach his master's side. Any enemy units no longer locked in combat as a result of this pile in move immediately consolidates. If Obyron is embarked on a transport or in a building when this special rule is triggered, ignore the normal rules for disembarkation – Obyron is simply removed from his current location and 'piled in' to Zahndrekh's combat.

'See, Obyron, the separatists come – attempting to outflank me just as they did at the Fourth Battle of Vyndakh. How they calculate that daubing themselves green and roaring like savages will produce a different outcome, I cannot fathom; but it is of no account.

Ready my legions – another glorious victory shall soon be ours.'

- Nemesor Zahndrekh to Vargard Obyron, prior to the crushing defeat of Waaagh! Bludtoof

ANRAKYR THE TRAVELLER

Few Necrons awaken from stasis-sleep with fully functioning consciousness. Most arise addled by the long slumber, their wits and reason slow to come fully online. Not so Anrakyr – he rose from dormancy with his mind intact and a great purpose foremost in his mind: to reunite the dynasties. Embracing this as his destiny, Anrakyr abdicated all responsibility to his own Tomb World of Pyrrhia and led an army into the stars.

Yet the galaxy has changed much since Anrakyr last walked its worlds, and the maps of old no longer correspond with the reality of the present. Planets have been destroyed, isolated by Warp storms or even shifted through time and space. Even should the world itself remain in the position recorded, the tomb beneath its surface might well be gone, destroyed by tectonic upheaval, meteor strike or other unforeseen disaster. Worst of all, however, is for Anrakyr to arrive upon a sleeping Tomb World to discover it infested with lesser life forms.

Anrakyr has little desire to start war for its own sake – his forces are too meagre for wanton hostility – but to arrive on a slumbering Tomb World to discover its catacombs collapsed and its resources plundered is enough to drive him into an abiding rage that bodes ill for the perpetrators. Be the invaders a low-tech colony, a sprawling Waaagh! of Orks, a Tau expeditionary force or the planet-choking industries of the Adeptus Mechanicus, only one response is possible: swift and absolute war – fighting alongside the Tomb World's forces if any remain, battling to avenge them if not. Not all the Tomb Worlds Anrakyr arrives upon are in such dire throes – some have gone entirely unnoticed by the younger races – but in a galaxy burgeoning with inquisitive life, such planets are few and far between.

From each Tomb World awoken or freed from invaders, Anrakyr requests a tithe of warriors and weaponry to be given over to his cause. If the supplication is refused, he seizes his prize through force or artifice instead. A newly awakened Tomb World is inevitably a confused and disordered place, and such acquisitions are easily engineered. This goes some way to explain Anrakyr's muddled repute amongst the Tomb Worlds he has encountered. To many nobles he is considered the highest avatar of nobility, a warrior who has yielded all ties of personal rank and status for the benefit of his people. To others, notably those who do not willingly contribute to his forces, Anrakyr is the worst kind of masterless brigand, almost as severe a threat to the slumbering Tomb Worlds as any of the galaxy's other perils. For his part, Anrakyr would prefer to be supported willingly, yet need overrides all. His forces, worn down and ravaged by campaign, are always on the brink of complete collapse, and without reinforcements his great cause would come swiftly to an end.

On the battlefield, Anrakyr is invariably accompanied by a cadre of his Pyrrhian Eternals – the remnant of the vast Immortal legion with which he began his great work. These ageless veterans are unswervingly loyal to their master and murderously efficient in furthering his goals. Yet even their threat pales beside that of Anrakyr himself. The same force of will that enables Anrakyr to maintain command over his forces can be refocused to deceive enemy targeting systems, granting him control of the foe's weaponry for brief periods of time. So it is that any foe who takes the field against Anrakyr would be well served to pay equal attention to the guns at their rear in addition to those at their front...

	WS	BS	S	T	W	I	A	Ld	Sv
Anrakyr the Traveller	4	4	5	5	3	2	3	10	3+

UNIT TYPE: Infantry (Character).

WARGEAR: Tachyon arrow, warscythe.

SPECIAL RULES: Counter-attack, Ever-living, Furious Charge, Independent Character, Reanimation Protocols.

Mind in the Machine: At the start of your Shooting phase, chose an enemy vehicle within 18" and in Anrakyr's line of sight and roll a D6. On a roll of 3+, Anrakyr overrides the targeting systems in that vehicle – you can immediately shoot with it as if it were your unit. The vehicle cannot alter its facing, and fires as if it had not moved. For the purposes of this attack, ignore any 'crew stunned' or 'crew shaken' results the target is suffering from – but destroyed weapons cannot be fired. Once these shooting attacks have been resolved, the vehicle returns to your opponent's control.

Pyrrhian Eternals: An army that includes Anrakyr the Traveller can also include a unit of Pyrrhian Eternals, as detailed in his army list entry. These are treated exactly as the Necron Immortals entry on page 34, save for the fact that these also have the Furious Charge and Counter-attack special rules.

> 'I am not capricious, nor am I given to cruel acts for their own sakes. It is simply a fact that you and your kind have trespassed, and thus invited extermination. Curse you for putting me to this inconvenience.'
>
> – Anrakyr the Traveller to Tau Ethereal Aun'taniel prior to the Harvest of Ka'mais

The Imperial Guardsmen behind the fortress walls had held firm so far, but now the time to strike had come. At Anrakyr's command, the Tomb Blades lanced forward, their tesla cannons sending great bolts of eldritch lightning arcing through the dug-in ranks of the Cadian 185th, carving bloody channels through the mass of men. The Tomb Blades made three passes before the fortress' flak towers had their measure, and even as a hail of high velocity autocannon shells blew the Necron craft out of the sky, Anrakyr had set the next phase of his attack in motion.

Emerging silently from the cover of the ruined city, a dozen Ghost Arks sailed down the freshly opened pathways through the wall of bayonets, skimming over the dead and dying to deliver punishing gauss broadsides at point-blank range. The Guardsmen were swept aside in disarray, allowing the sinister vessels to disgorge squad after squad of Necron Warriors in the midst of the wavering Cadians.

Only then did Anrakyr unleash the third attack wave: a legion of his own Pyrrhian Eternals, the finest Immortals in the galaxy, augmented at the hands of the twisted Cryptek, Szeras. In perfect unison, they marched into the teeth of the Imperial Guard lines, las-fire and heavy bolter shells ricocheting off their armour. Anrakyr led that charge, hacking his way toward an Imperial Guard officer, who stood tall beneath his regimental colours. Anrakyr was no more than twenty paces from his target when a deafening explosion tore through the Pyrrhian Eternals' ranks, blowing a dozen Immortals to pieces and knocking the Overlord unceremoniously into the mud. As Anrakyr hauled himself to his feet, he caught sight of his assailant: a Leman Russ battle tank, whose turret was even then coming to bear for another shot.

Reaching out his consciousness to the rudimentary spirit of the Leman Russ, Anrakyr saw that the tank was intended to be a masterpiece of design. But he saw also that technological incompetents had made alterations that had served only to cage the Leman Russ's full efficiency. How fitting then, that this abused machine would now take a measure of revenge upon its tormentors. Tightening his mental grip, Anrakyr seized control of the tank's weapon systems – even technology so basic could not resist his will – and fired point-blank into the Cadian colour party, tearing them to red ruin. A moment later, the systems overloaded completely, bringing the tank to a lifeless halt.

With the death of their officer, the heart went out of the Cadians, and the rout began. Yet so completely had the Guardsmen been surrounded that few survived to reach the fortress gates. When Szeras found him, Anrakyr stood in the shadow of the disabled Leman Russ, delicately running the fingers of one hand over the seized-up behemoth's armour plates as he appraised the battle yet to come.

'The augmentations to your Immortals are performing exactly as projected,' the Cryptek informed his master, 'but an assault will inevitably incur heavy losses.'

Anrakyr replied without turning. 'The contingency might yet not arise. The codes of battle allow me to extend the option of honourable surrender to their commander. We require neither their destruction, nor that of the fortress. Access to the catacombs beneath is our only priority.'

'He will not accede,' Szeras intoned, 'Every delay is a moment in which his reinforcements draw closer.'

'Nonetheless, this is the proper protocol. The commander and his men have fought well, for primitives. The offer is to be extended.'

'Unnecessary,' Szeras stated, his gaze shifting. Turning, Anrakyr saw a shadow fall over the fortress. When it had passed, the defenders were no longer alone. Scores of hooded hunters had materialised amongst the fortress's flak towers and sensor arrays. With keen blades that clove metal like flesh, they silenced the defence turrets, and with synaptic disintegrators, they scoured guardsmen from the ramparts. Eyes blazing, Anrakyr rounded on Szeras. 'Deathmarks? I gave no such command.'

'The instruction was mine. Your course held flaws.' Szeras replied. Anrakyr gripped his warscythe tightly, but said nothing as he watched the massacre play out. Trapped within the tomb-like walls of their own fortress, the Guardsmen were soon slaughtered. Scant minutes later, the great gate of the fortress opened. In frosty silence, Overlord and Cryptek strode inside.

As Anrakyr stepped through the gates, the Deathmarks assembled in the courtyard sank to their knees, gazes averted. The only being who remained standing was a solitary prisoner, his colonel's uniform blackened and matted with blood, and he quivered with defiant rage and barely controlled terror. Anrakyr gave the slightest of bows before speaking. 'Adversary,' he paused, searching for the correct word, 'Colonel. You have fought well. No shame should be inferred from this defeat.' In response, the captive spat full in the towering Overlord's face.

'You've won nothing here. More armies will come, and they will destroy you in the Emperor's name.'

'Is that so?' Anrakyr replied evenly, and brought his warscythe about to strike the colonel's head from his shoulders. As the decapitated corpse toppled to the ground, Szeras spoke, his voice tinged with outrage. 'How dare you! He was to have been mine. That was our accord: my aid in exchange for him: alive. This is outrageo...'

'You forget your station, Cryptek,' Anrakyr interrupted, his voice as chill as the night air. 'Your payment was forfeit from the moment you manipulated the battle's prosecution, an error compounded through improper method. Your services are necessary, but I shall abide neither your insubordination, nor your impertinence. Be gone from my sight.' Szeras, knowing better than to openly issue further challenge to the Overlord, stalked away.

'As for you,' Anrakyr continued, now addressing the silent ranks of Deathmarks, 'Leave this place. The one who called you here had no authority to do so. Do not return unbidden.' The Deathmarks made no reply, but a moment later, coiling shadows consumed them, and when the darkness dispersed like smoke on a midnight breeze, the Deathmarks were gone. Suppressing his anger, Anrakyr returned to the matter at hand. The battle was over, but there were still many challenges to overcome if the Tomb World of Kaldrakh was to be returned to wakefulness...

AWAKENING THE TOMB

The Necron army once conquered the galaxy, and in your hands it can do so again. With their arcane technologies, formidable firepower and ability to self-repair, the Necrons are an army worthy of any foe's respect.

GETTING STARTED

With all armies, it's important to understand their strengths and weaknesses, and Necrons are no exception. Their biggest advantage is their durability. All Necrons have a high Toughness, a good armour save and most have a Reanimation Protocols 'save' that gives them a chance of returning to play even after they have been destroyed. As a result, they are incredibly resilient, able to inflict and endure a punishing amount of firepower.

However, beware the assault! Due to their low Initiative values, Necrons often find themselves overmatched in close combat and, whilst their innate resilience goes some way to countering this, Necrons locked in melee are often Necrons about to be removed as casualties (though there are a few exceptions, such as Flayed Ones, Lychguard and Triarch Praetorians). With all this in mind, as a Necron player you should always be seeking to engage your foes at range – the better to bring your overwhelming firepower to bear.

SUMMON THE LEGIONS

First of all, you'll need to choose an HQ character to lead your army. For your first few games, it's best to head up your force with a Necron Overlord. This ancient warrior might be slow to strike, but he'll almost certainly be stronger and tougher than his opposite number in the enemy army. Using your Necron Overlord to reinforce an advance or a desperate defence can make the difference between victory and defeat. You may also consider upgrading your Overlord to a Phaeron, giving him and his unit the Relentless special and allowing them to stride implacably across the battlefield whilst not sacrificing any of their firepower.

Whichever HQ unit you choose, it's also worth considering a Royal Court – a bodyguard of Crypteks and Necron Lords. This is a formidable unit in its own right, but also offers you a bit of versatility. At the start of the game, Lords and Crypteks from the Royal Court can be split off to join other units in your army, boosting their combat potential.

FORMING THE PHALANX

But enough about the leaders of your army – let's talk about the units that are going to win the game for you: the Troops. Necron Warriors and Immortals are the soulless heart of any Necron army, and you're going to need plenty of them. Both are primarily anti-infantry units but, thanks to the unique properties of gauss weapons, they can also threaten tanks if their numbers are large enough.

Once you've sorted out the core of your army, it's time to think about the specialist squads you'll be fielding in support of your Troops. There's plenty of choice to be had here, depending on whether you want to make a sprawling force or a more tightly-packed, elite army. If you're wanting to boost your numbers, it's hard to go wrong with Deathmarks,

Tomb Blades and Flayed Ones (for extra shooting power, speed and close combat potential respectively). Conversely, if you want to fill your ranks out with expensive heavy-hitting shock troops, you'll want to look at the ethereal might of the C'tan Shards, the unstoppable close combat power of the Lychguard or the versatile Triarch Praetorians.

ANCIENT ARMOUR

As a Necron player, your infantry will carry you a long way, but you'll go further with a few vehicles to back you up. Just like the Necrons themselves, Necron vehicles are incredibly tough. Living Metal allows them a chance to resist 'crew shaken' and 'crew stunned' results, and many craft also have quantum shields that dramatically increase their survivability.

As to which vehicles you add to your force, that depends on the role you want them to perform. The Doomsday Ark, Triarch Stalker and Doom Scythe place plenty of all-purpose firepower at your disposal, and are often the best way of getting some dedicated anti-vehicle weaponry onto the battlefield. Elsewhere, the Ghost Ark, Night Scythe and Monolith present options for getting your forces swiftly around the tabletop – either through conventional transportation, or eerie teleportation. These vehicles can be crucial for getting your forces onto objectives, or setting up ambushes on advancing foes.

ARISE, THE ROBOTS

Last but not least, we come to the robot servitors of the Tomb Worlds, the Canoptek Spyders, Wraiths and Scarabs. These three units are specialists, and they bring unique abilities to the battlefield. Take Canoptek Scarabs, for example. While you can take them in large enough numbers to overwhelm enemies in close combat, what you really need them for is to chew through the armour on enemy tanks. Similarly, a Canoptek Spyder is no pushover in close combat, but you'll often find it's far better employed repairing your own damaged vehicles. Canoptek Wraiths, on the other hand, are excellent advance troops. They're too much of a threat for your opponent to ignore; pitch them into the fray as quickly as possible – whilst the foe are busy trying to down the Wraiths, the rest of your army is advancing unimpeded.

Ultimately, the Necron army offers an almost infinite amount of tactical choice. After a few games, you'll establish what play style suits you best, and refine your army composition. From that moment on, rule of the galaxy is within your grasp!

> 'Our armies are the most finely crafted of all our machines, and like all machines, each component, however small, has its function. Act within established parameters, and there is no force in the galaxy that can stand before you. Operate outside them, and you concede defeat.'
>
> - Imotekh the Stormlord

The sands of a long-dormant crownworld give up their dead, and the Necron Legions advance to war.

Trazyn the Infinite

Imotekh the Stormlord

Necron Overlord

Necron Lord

Imotekh the Stormlord leads a phalanx of Lychguard into battle.

Cryptek

Destroyer Lords exist only to slaughter the living.

Necron Overlords often survey the battlefield from Catacomb Command Barges.

Awakening the Tomb

Necron Warriors armed with gauss flayers

Necron Warriors

Necron Warrior from the
Mephrit Dynasty

Necron Warrior from the
Nephrekh Dynasty

Necron Warrior in service to the
Agdagath Dynasty

Necron Warrior from the
Thokt Dynasty

Warrior, Immortal and Lychguard from the Charnovokh Dynasty

This Warrior, Immortal and Lychguard bear the blood-red heraldry of the Novokh Dynasty.

The scions of the Nihilakh Dynasty arise to reclaim the lost Tomb World of Kephnerakh.

Awakening the Tomb

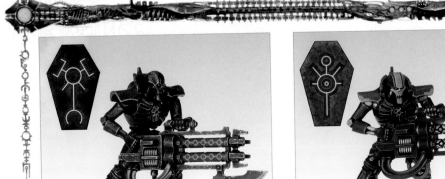

Immortal from the Nekthyst Dynasty

Immortal from the Nephrekh Dynasty

The Ankh of the Triarch – this royal symbol is used by all Necron Dynasties.

Immortals armed with gauss blasters

Immortals indentured to the Sautekh Dynasty

Immortal from the Thokt Dynasty

Immortals with tesla carbines

The overwhelming might of the Lychguard sweeps aside the Ultramarines.

Lychguards armed with hyperphase swords and dispersion shields

Lychguard from the Ogdobekh Dynasty

Lychguards armed with warscythes

Lychguard from the Charnovokh Dynasty

Awakening the Tomb

Triarch Praetorians are brutal close-quarters fighters.

Triarch Praetorian with rod of covenant

Triarch Praetorian armed with particle caster and voidblade

Deathmarks armed with synaptic disintegrators

Deathmark from the Sekemtar Dynasty

Deathmarks are expert assassins who appear without warning amidst the enemy lines.

Deathmark from the Atun Dynasty

Awakening the Tomb

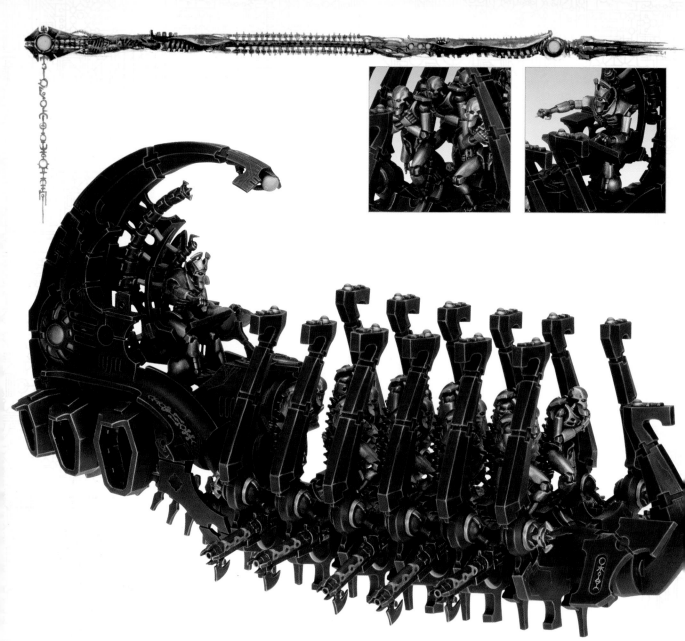

Ghost Arks ferry Necron Warriors to the battlefront and repair those that have fallen.

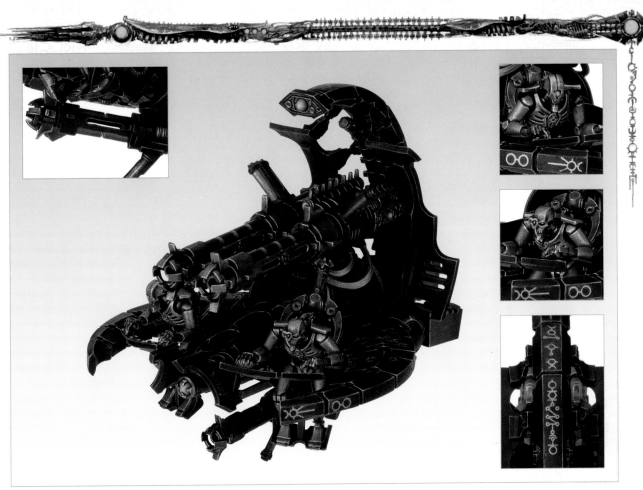

Annihilation Barge

C'tan Shard of the Nightbringer

C'tan Shard of the Deceiver

Awakening the Tomb

Flayed Ones are ghoulish feasters on the dead.

Necron Destroyer

Icon of the
Nihilakh Dynasty

Icon of the
Sarnekh Dynasty

Necron Heavy Destroyer

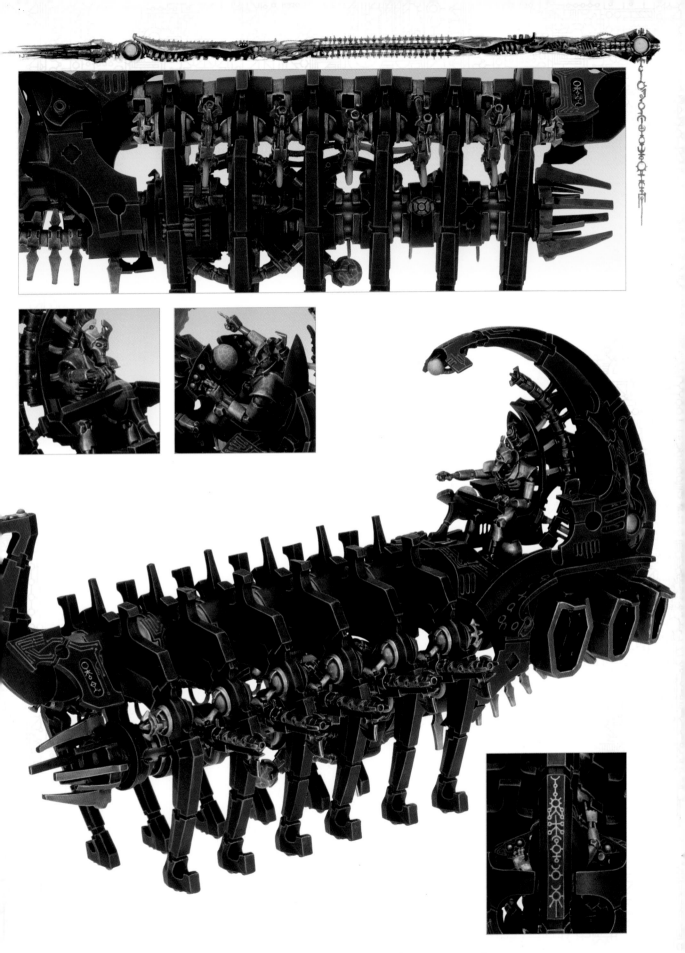

The Doomsday Ark is the most fearsome weapon in the Necrons' arsenal.

A remorseless Necron legion stalks through the ruins of an Imperial city.

Under the command of Overlord Kepakh, the forces of the Nihilakh Dynasty launch their reconquest of the galaxy.

NECRON WARGEAR

This section of Codex: Necrons lists all the weapons and equipment employed by the Necrons, along with the rules for using them in your games of Warhammer 40,000.

You'll find all the Necron weapons and equipment listed in this section. Most such wargear also has its rules presented here, though a few highly specialised items are contained on the relevant page in the Army of Aeons Past section.

Not all pieces of wargear presented here are used by more than one unit. Some are collated here with other weapons of a similar type for ease of reference. Of special note are the items of wargear used by Crypteks, which have a section of their own on pages 84-85.

If you need to consult the rules for a particular piece of Necron wargear, check this section first – even if the item in question isn't detailed here, you'll find a page reference for it at the end of the Weapons and Equipment section.

'Superior technology does not guarantee victory unless wielded by a superior being.'

- Illuminor Szeras

WEAPONS AND EQUIPMENT

GAUNTLET OF FIRE

The gauntlet of fire takes the form of an armoured glove and vambrace, whose length crackles and flows with green flame. The gauntlet's mechanisms are controlled by a series of submechadermal filaments, allowing the wielder a level of control over the gauntlet as fine as over his own hand.

A gauntlet of fire is a close combat weapon. Attacks made with a gauntlet of fire re-roll failed rolls To Hit and To Wound in close combat. The gauntlet of fire can also shoot with the following profile:

Range	Str	AP	Type
Template	4	5	Assault 1

GAUSS WEAPONS

Gauss-type weapons are the most common of all guns carried by the Necron soldiery and vary in appearance from the rifle-sized gauss flayer through to the massive heavy gauss cannon. Unlike more conventional energy weapons, a gauss projector does not deliver a cutting beam or bolt of force. Instead it emits a molecular disassembling beam, capable of reducing flesh, armour and bone to constituent atoms.

'Gauss' type:

Any armour penetration roll made by weapon with the Gauss type will score a glancing hit on a D6 roll of 6, unless the dice roll is already sufficient to cause a penetrating hit.

	Range	Str	AP	Type
Gauss flayer	24"	4	5	Rapid Fire, Gauss
Gauss blaster	24"	5	4	Rapid Fire, Gauss
Gauss cannon	24"	5	3	Assault 2, Gauss
Heavy gauss cannon	36"	9	2	Assault 1, Gauss
Gauss flux arc	24"	4	5	Heavy 3, Gauss*

A Gauss flux arc can be fired at a different target unit to other weapons on the vehicle (including other gauss flux arcs) subject to the normal rules for shooting.

HYPERPHASE SWORD

The energy blade of a hyperphase sword vibrates across dimensional states, and can easily slice through armour and flesh to sever vital organs within.

A hyperphase sword is a power weapon.

MINDSHACKLE SCARABS

Mindshackle scarabs are one of the Necrons' chief methods of controlling alien races. At the bearer's command, tiny scarabs bury into the victim's mind and bypass cerebral functions, turning the victim into little more than a puppet under the control of the scarabs' master.

At the start of the Assault phase, after assault moves have been made, but before any blows are struck, randomly select an enemy model in base contact with the bearer of the mindshackle scarabs. That model must immediately take a Leadership test on 3D6. If the test is passed, the mindshackle scarabs have no effect. If the test is failed, the victim strikes out at his allies. Instead of attacking normally, he inflicts D3 hits on his own unit when it is his turn to attack. These hits are resolved at the victim's Strength, and benefit from any abilities and penalties from his close combat weapons (the controller of the mindshackle scarabs chooses which, if there is a choice). If he is still alive, the victim returns to normal once all blows in that round of combat have been struck.

PARTICLE WEAPONS

These weapons emit a stream of miniscule anti-matter particles that detonate on contact with other matter. They are incredibly reliable, needing only enough energy to maintain the containment field that prevents the anti-matter detonating within the weapons' mechanism.

	Range	Str	AP	Type
Particle caster	12"	6	5	Pistol
Particle beamer	24"	6	5	Heavy 1, Blast
Particle shredder	24"	7	4	Heavy 1, Large Blast
Particle whip	24"	8	3	Ordnance 1, Large Blast

PHASE SHIFTER

A phase shifter flickers its bearer into and out of a phased state. If improperly timed, blows and shots aimed at the bearer of the phase shifter instead pass through empty air.

A model with a phase shifter has a 3+ invulnerable save.

PHYLACTERY

This inconspicuous charm is a powerful self-repair device, filled with tiny, spider-like creatures that swarm over the bearer's wounds, re-knitting his ravaged body.

One use only. A model with a phylactery that passes his first Reanimation Protocols roll returns to play with D3 Wounds.

QUANTUM SHIELDING

Necron quantum shielding defies examination, for it exists only at the moment of deflection – at all other times there is no indication of its presence.

Until the vehicle suffers a penetrating hit, it counts all Armour Values on its front and side facings as being 2 points higher. Once the vehicle has suffered a penetrating hit, it uses its own armour value against subsequent hits.

RESURRECTION ORB

This glowing sphere focuses energy into the regeneration circuits of surrounding Necrons, hastening their repair.

The bearer of the resurrection orb (and his unit) pass Reanimation Protocols rolls on a 4+.

SEMPITERNAL WEAVE

Many a Necron Lord's exoskeleton is threaded with filaments of phase-hardened amaranthite and adamantium, vastly increasing their hardiness.

A model with sempiternal weave has a 2+ armour save.

STAFF OF LIGHT

The staff of light is both a weapon and a symbol of authority. Its haft is actually a disguised power generator rod, and the crest a finely tuned focussing device, allowing the wielder to unleash searing bolts of energy at his foes.

A staff of light is a shooting weapon with the following profile:

Range	Str	AP	Type
12"	5	3	Assault 3

> 'Your desires are irrelevant. This galaxy once knelt before us, and it will do so again.'
>
> - Overlord Akanabekh
> Phaeron of the Kardenath Dynasty
> Regent of Nagathar

TACHYON ARROW

The tachyon arrow is an intricate wrist-mounted energy caster. When activated, it transmutes a sliver of inert metal into an unstoppable thunderbolt capable of piercing the heart of a mountain.

The tachyon arrow allows the bearer to make the following shooting attack once per game:

Range	Str	AP	Type
∞ (Infinite)	10	1	Assault 1

TESLA WEAPONS

A tesla weapon unleashes a bolt of living lightning that crackles from foe to foe after hitting its target, charring flesh and melting armour. Tesla bolts feed off the energy released by the destruction, the lightning becoming more furious with every fresh arc.

'Tesla' type:

Tesla shots have a chance to strike several times with a single shot. For every To Hit roll of 6, the target suffers 2 additional automatic hits.

	Range	Str	AP	Type
Tesla carbine	24"	5	-	Assault 1, Tesla
Tesla cannon	24"	6	-	Assault 2, Tesla
Tesla destructor	24"	7	-	Assault 4, Tesla, Arc

Arc: Once the tesla destructor's initial shot has been resolved, roll a D6 for each other unit (friendly and enemy, engaged and unengaged) within 6" of the target. If you roll a 6, that unit suffers D6 automatic Strength 5, AP - hits.

TESSERACT LABYRINTH

A tesseract labyrinth is the physical manifestation of a pocket-dimensional prison gateway. Once caught within its folds, there can be no escape.

One use only. The bearer can use the tesseract labyrinth in lieu of making close combat attacks that round. Choose a character or monstrous creature in base contact with the bearer. The victim must immediately roll equal to or under its remaining Wounds on a D6 or be trapped within the tesseract labyrinth forever. Remove as a casualty with no saves of any kind allowed.

TRANSDIMENSIONAL BEAMER

Used as a convenient method of banishing unwanted debris, machinery and failed experiments from Tomb Worlds and battlefields into a pocket dimension, the transdimensional beamer can just as easily be used to banish foes.

Range	Str	AP	Type
12"	X	-	Heavy 1, Exile Ray

Exile Ray: If a shot from a weapon with the exile ray type hits, randomly select a model in the target unit. That model must immediately pass a Strength test or be removed as a casualty with no saves of any kind allowed. Models with no Strength value automatically pass.

VOIDBLADE

The gleaming black edge of a voidblade flickers in and out of existence, causing molecular bonds to disintegrate in any foe unfortunate enough to be struck.

A voidblade is a close combat weapon with the Rending and Entropic Strike special rules.

WARSCYTHES

Warscythes are energy-bladed battle-staves – the favoured weapons of Necron Lords and their bodyguards for many thousands of years. A warscythe is incredibly heavy and cumbersome. In the hands of a lesser creature it would be of little threat, but when wielded by the tireless mechanical musculature of a Necron, it is a most formidable weapon.

A warscythe is a two-handed close combat weapon. Attacks made with a warscythe are resolved with a +2 Strength bonus. Additionally, hits with a warscythe roll 2D6 for Armour Penetration. Armour saves are not permitted against Wounds caused by a warscythe.

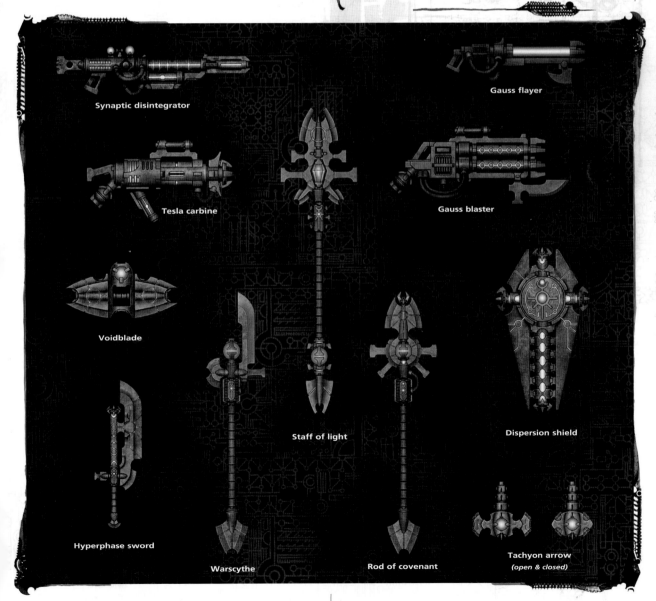

Synaptic disintegrator

Gauss flayer

Tesla carbine

Gauss blaster

Voidblade

Staff of light

Dispersion shield

Hyperphase sword

Warscythe

Rod of covenant

Tachyon arrow
(open & closed)

CRYPTEK WARGEAR

The disciplines of techno-sorcery are wide and varied. It is rare for two Crypteks to evince exactly the same abilities, but for the purposes of games of Warhammer 40,000, we can assume that they fall into several broad categories of effect. Presented here are items of wargear tied to the five most common techno-sorcery disciplines. As presented in the army list, no Cryptek can mix wargear from two or more disciplines – such a thing is almost entirely unheard of as it indicates a most untrustworthy or undisciplined mind.

HARBINGERS OF DESPAIR

Accomplished psychomancers are amongst the most keenly retained of all Crypteks. If their abilities are properly employed, the enemy's morale will be shattered within moments of the battle's start.

ABYSSAL STAFF

To succumb to the swirling ebon mists called by the abyssal staff is to be swallowed in impenetrable madness.

This is a shooting weapon with the following profile:

	Range	Str	AP	Type
Abyssal staff	Template	8	1	Assault 1, Shroud of Despair

Shroud of Despair: *To Wound rolls from the abyssal staff's shooting attacks are made against the target's Leadership, rather than Toughness. The abyssal staff's shooting attack has no effect against vehicles.*

NIGHTMARE SHROUD

Unveiling the nightmare shroud assails nearby enemies with phantasms of dread as potent as any mortal danger.

The nightmare shroud can be used during the Shooting phase instead of firing a weapon. Choose an unengaged enemy unit within 18" of the Cryptek. That unit must immediately take a Morale check.

VEIL OF DARKNESS

The Cryptek can summon a veil of darkness which twists and billows like a ghostly cloak blown by an ethereal breeze. When the darkness ebbs, the Cryptek and his comrades have disappeared, only to rematerialise some distance away.

A Cryptek with a veil of darkness can use it in its Movement phase instead of moving normally. The Cryptek and his unit are removed from the tabletop and immediately Deep Strike back onto the battlefield. The veil of darkness cannot be used if the Cryptek or his unit are locked in combat.

HARBINGERS OF DESTRUCTION

Plasmancers are not subtle beings, for they choose to wield raw energy rather than go to the trouble of binding it into other forms. Thus are they know as Harbingers of Destruction, as that is their gift to the galaxy.

ELDRITCH LANCE

This stave can emit a blast of furious energy whose passage makes even the air scream in agony.

This is a shooting weapon with the following profile:

	Range	Str	AP	Type
Eldritch lance	36"	8	2	Assault 1

GAZE OF FLAME

Flickering witch-fires blaze from the Cryptek's eyes, faltering the onset of even the bravest attacker.

The Cryptek, and his unit, are treated as being armed with defensive grenades. The rest of the unit loses this ability if the Cryptek is removed as a casualty.

SOLAR PULSE

The Cryptek's staff unleashes a flash of searing light, blinding his enemies and illuminating the battlefield.

One use only. The solar pulse can be used at the start of any turn. If the Night Fighting rules are in effect, they cease to apply until the end of the turn. If the Night Fighting rules are not in effect, then they apply until the end of the turn.

HARBINGERS OF ETERNITY

Chronomancers are known as Harbingers of Eternity, as knowledge of the future flows through their every act. Few Harbingers of Eternity are trusted, as they always have a shrewd idea of how any event will unfold.

AEONSTAVE

The sapphire head of an aeonstave contains a massive chronal charge that, when unleashed, can trap a foe in a bubble of slow-time.

The aeonstave is a close combat weapon. Any enemy that suffers an unsaved Wound from an aeonstave loses the Fleet special rule (if he has it) and has his Weapon Skill, Ballistic Skill, Initiative and Attacks values reduced to 1 for the remainder of the game.

CHRONOMETRON

The chronometron allows the bearer to act out of phase from the normal time flow, permitting him to make minor, but sometimes potent, alterations to his destiny.

A model with a chronometron can re-roll one of his D6 rolls each phase. If the bearer is in a unit, this ability can be used to instead re-roll one of the unit's D6 rolls each phase.

TIMESPLINTER CLOAK

The Cryptek is encased in shards of crystallised time, each splinter proof against any blow not landed in the split-second formed in another moment.

A model with a timesplinter cloak has a 3+ invulnerable save.

HARBINGERS OF THE STORM

Harbingers of the Storm are ethermancers, with the fury of the turbulent skies at their command. They can summon lightning, or set enraged winds upon the foe.

ETHER CRYSTAL

Still air comes to howling life in the presence of an ether crystal, buffeting the Cryptek's enemies with crushing pressure waves and bolts of lightning.

Any enemy unit arriving by Deep Strike within 6" of the bearer of an ether crystal suffers D6 Strength 8 AP 5 hits. If any enemy unit arrives by Deep Strike within range of one or more ether crystals, then increase the number of hits by one for each ether crystal beyond the first (it doesn't suffer D6 hits per ether crystal).

LIGHTNING FIELD

Bolts of emerald lightning arc between the Cryptek and his comrades, electrocuting any foe who comes near.

When an enemy unit successfully moves into assault with the Cryptek (or his unit) the assaulting unit immediately suffers D6 Strength 8, AP 5 hits. The rest of the unit loses this ability if the Cryptek is removed as a casualty.

VOLTAIC STAFF

Just as the ethermancer commands the voltaic staff, so does the voltaic staff command the lightning.

This is a shooting weapon with the following profile:

	Range	Str	AP	Type
Voltaic staff	12"	5	-	Assault 4, Haywire

Haywire: *Vehicles hit by a shot from the voltaic staff suffer a glancing hit on a 2-5, and a penetrating hit on a 6.*

HARBINGERS OF TRANSMOGRIFICATION

Harbingers of Transmogrifcation are adepts of geomancy and masters of the science once known as alchemy. They specialise in the transmutation of matter from one form to another and the instilling of animus in the inanimate.

HARP OF DISSONANCE

A single booming bass note from these electrum strings can transform adamantium plate to a brittle glass.

	Range	Str	AP	Type
Harp of dissonance	∞ (Infinite)	6	-	Assault 1, Entropic Strike

SEISMIC CRUCIBLE

The bearer of a seismic crucible can induce localised tremors in rock, metal and even the air itself.

At the start of the enemy Assault phase, roll a D3 and nominate an enemy unit. If the nominated unit attempts to assault the Cryptek, or his unit, reduce their assault move by the result of the D3 for that phase.

TREMORSTAVE

The energy blast from a tremorstave causes shards of rock to burst from the ground, knocking any survivors sprawling.

This is a shooting weapon with the following profile:

	Range	Str	AP	Type
Tremorstave	36"	4	-	Assault 1, Blast, Quake

Quake: *All enemy units hit by a weapon with the Quake type treat open ground as difficult terrain during their next Movement phase.*

STRANGE SCIENCES

Necrons were ever masters of transcendent physics, pocket dimensions and hyper-geometry, and these sciences are put to full effect wherever they can serve useful function. Many Tomb Worlds and strongholds are far more vast within than they might appear from the outside, or are protected by energy labyrinths of impossible size. Some specialised troops, notably Deathmarks, regularly employ pocket dimensions as vantage points from which to hunt their foes, and the more accomplished nemesors can conceal entire armies and fleets in slivers of out-of-phase reality. Yet, as confounding as these techniques might be to the other races of the galaxy, there is one enemy against whom they are no defence. To the Daemons of the Warp, such technological conjurings are merely another flavour of existence to be corrupted and devoured.

NECRON ARMY LIST

The following army list enables you to field an army of Necrons and fight battles using the scenarios included in the *Warhammer 40,000* rulebook.

USING THE ARMY LIST

The Necron army list is split into five sections: HQ, Elites, Troops, Fast Attack and Heavy Support. All of the squads, vehicles and characters in the army are placed into one of these sections depending upon their role on the battlefield. Each model is also given a points value that varies depending on how effective that model is in battle.

Before you choose an army, you will need to agree with your opponent upon the type of game you are going to play and the maximum total number of points each of you will spend. Then you can proceed to pick your army.

USING A FORCE ORGANISATION CHART

The army list is used in conjunction with the Force Organisation chart from a scenario. Each chart is split into five categories that correspond to the sections in the army list, and each category has one or more boxes. Each grey-toned box indicates that you may make one choice from that section of the army list, while a dark-toned box indicates a compulsory selection.

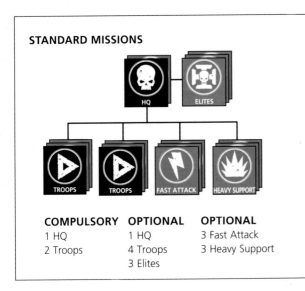

STANDARD MISSIONS

COMPULSORY	OPTIONAL	OPTIONAL
1 HQ	1 HQ	3 Fast Attack
2 Troops	4 Troops	3 Heavy Support
	3 Elites	

'I have slain gods, toppled empires and destroyed entire worlds. Compared to this, your meagre death will likely go unnoticed by history, but do not despair, little hero – I shall always remember this moment.'

— *Anrakyr the Traveller*

ARMY LIST ENTRIES

Each entry in the army list represents a different unit. More information about the background and rules for the Necrons and their options can be found in the Army of Aeons Past section, while examples of the Citadel miniatures you will need to represent them can be found in the Awakening the Tomb section.

Each unit entry in the Necron army list is split into several sections:

Name: At the start of each army list entry you will find the name of the unit alongside the point's cost of the unit without any upgrades.

Profile: This section will show the characteristics profile of any models the unit can include.

Composition: Where applicable, this section will show the number and type of models that make up the basic unit, before any upgrades are taken. If the Unit Composition includes the word 'Unique', then you may only include one of this unit in your army.

Unit Type: This refers to the Unit Type Rules chapter of the *Warhammer 40,000* rulebook. For example, a unit may be classed as infantry, vehicle or cavalry, which will subject it to a number of rules regarding movement, shooting, assault, etc.

Wargear: This section details the weapons and equipment the models in the unit are armed with. The cost for all these models and their equipment is included in the points cost listed next to the unit name.

Special Rules: Any special rules that apply to the models in the unit are listed here. These special rules are explained in further detail in either the Army of Aeons Past section or the *Warhammer 40,000* rulebook.

Dedicated Transport: Where applicable, this section refers to any transport vehicles the unit may take. These have their own army list entry on page 91. Dedicated transports do not use up any Force Organisation chart selections, but otherwise function as separate units. The Transport Vehicles section of the *Warhammer 40,000* rulebook, and their entry in this book, explains how these dedicated transport vehicles work.

Options: This section lists all of the upgrades you may add to the unit, should you wish to do so, alongside the associated points cost for each. Where an option states that you may exchange one weapon 'and/or' another, you may replace either, neither or both, provided you pay the points cost.

HQ

IMOTEKH THE STORMLORD .... 225 points

Page 54

	WS	BS	S	T	W	I	A	Ld	Sv
Imotekh the Stormlord	4	4	5	5	3	2	3	10	2+

Wargear:
- Bloodswarm nanoscarabs
- Gauntlet of fire
- Phase shifter
- Phylactery
- Sempiternal weave
- Staff of the Destroyer

Special Rules:
- Ever-living
- Humiliating Defeat
- Hyperlogical Strategy
- Independent Character
- Lord of the Storm
- Phaeron
- Reanimation Protocols

Composition:
- 1 (Unique)

Unit Type:
- Infantry (Character)

Dedicated Transport:
- May select a Catacomb Command Barge as a dedicated transport (see page 91 for points costs).

NEMESOR ZAHNDREKH .... 185 points

Page 60

	WS	BS	S	T	W	I	A	Ld	Sv
Nemesor Zahndrekh	4	4	5	5	3	2	3	10	2+

Wargear:
- Phase shifter
- Resurrection orb
- Sempiternal weave
- Staff of light

Special Rules:
- Adaptive Tactics
- Counter Tactics
- Ever-living
- Independent Character
- Phased Reinforcements
- Reanimation Protocols

Composition:
- 1 (Unique)

Unit Type:
- Infantry (Character)

Dedicated Transport:
- May select a Catacomb Command Barge as a dedicated transport (see page 91 for points costs).

VARGARD OBYRON .... 160 points

Page 60

Vargard Obyron does not take up an HQ choice if your army also includes Nemesor Zahndrekh

	WS	BS	S	T	W	I	A	Ld	Sv
Vargard Obyron	6	4	5	5	3	2	3	10	2+

Wargear:
- Ghostwalk mantle
- Sempiternal weave
- Warscythe

Special Rules:
- Cleaving Counterblow
- Ever-living
- Independent Character
- Reanimation Protocols
- The Vargard's Duty

Composition:
- 1 (Unique)

Unit Type:
- Infantry (Character)

ILLUMINOR SZERAS .... 100 points

Page 56

	WS	BS	S	T	W	I	A	Ld	Sv
Illuminor Szeras	4	4	4	4	2	2	4	10	3+

Wargear:
- Eldritch lance
- Gaze of flame

Special Rules:
- Ever-living
- Independent Character
- Mechanical Augmentation
- Reanimation Protocols

Composition:
- 1 (Unique)

Unit Type:
- Infantry (Character)

ORIKAN THE DIVINER .... 165 points

Page 57

	WS	BS	S	T	W	I	A	Ld	Sv
Orikan the Diviner	4	4	4	4	2	2	2	10	4+
Orikan Empowered	5	5	7	7	4	4	4	10	4+

Wargear:
- Phase Shifter
- Staff of Tomorrow
- Transdimensional beamer

Special Rules:
- Ever-living
- Independent Character
- Lord of Time
- Temporal Snares
- Reanimation Protocols
- The Stars Are Right

Composition:
- 1 (Unique)

Unit Type:
- Infantry (Character)

HQ

ANRAKYR THE TRAVELLER .... 165 points

	WS	BS	S	T	W	I	A	Ld	Sv
Anrakyr the Traveller	4	4	5	5	3	2	3	10	3+

Composition:
- 1 (Unique)

Unit Type:
- Infantry (Character)

Wargear:
- Tachyon arrow
- Warscythe

Special Rules:
- Counter-attack
- Ever-living
- Furious Charge
- Independent Character
- Mind in the Machine
- Reanimation Protocols

Dedicated Transport:
- May select a Catacomb Command Barge as a dedicated transport (see page 91 for points costs).

Pyrrhian Eternals:
- If your army includes Anrakyr the Traveller, one unit of Immortals is automatically upgraded to Pyrrhian Eternals at no additional cost (see page 62).

TRAZYN THE INFINITE .... 175 points

Page 58

	WS	BS	S	T	W	I	A	Ld	Sv
Trazyn the Infinite	4	4	5	5	3	2	3	10	3+

Composition:
- 1 (Unique)

Unit Type:
- Infantry (Character)

Wargear:
- Empathic obliterator
- Mindshackle scarabs

Special Rules:
- Ever-living
- 'Excellent! Another Piece for the Collection'
- Independent Character
- Phaeron
- Reanimation Protocols
- Surrogate Hosts

Dedicated Transport:
- May select a Catacomb Command Barge as a dedicated transport (see page 91 for points costs).

NECRON OVERLORD .... 90 points

Page 30

	WS	BS	S	T	W	I	A	Ld	Sv
Necron Overlord	4	4	5	5	3	2	3	10	3+

Composition:
- 1 Necron Overlord

Unit Type:
- Infantry (Character)

Wargear:
- Staff of light

Special Rules:
- Ever-living
- Independent Character
- Reanimation Protocols

Dedicated Transport:
- May select a Catacomb Command Barge as a dedicated transport (see page 91 for points costs).

Options:
- Upgrade to Phaeron .... 20 points
- May exchange staff of light for one of the following:
  - Hyperphase sword .... free
  - Gauntlet of fire .... 5 points
  - Voidblade .... 10 points
  - Warscythe .... 10 points
- May take any of the following:
  - Phylactery .... 15 points
  - Mindshackle scarabs .... 15 points
  - Sempiternal weave .... 15 points
  - Tesseract labyrinth .... 20 points
  - Tachyon arrow .... 30 points
  - Resurrection orb .... 30 points
  - Phase shifter .... 45 points

DESTROYER LORD .... 125 points

Page 31

	WS	BS	S	T	W	I	A	Ld	Sv
Destroyer Lord	4	4	5	6	3	2	3	10	3+

Composition:
- 1 Destroyer Lord

Unit Type:
- Jump Infantry (Character)

Wargear:
- Warscythe

Special Rules:
- Ever-living
- Independent Character
- Preferred Enemy (Everything!)
- Reanimation Protocols

Options:
- May exchange warscythe for one of the following:
  - Gauntlet of fire .... free
  - Staff of light .... free
  - Voidblade .... 5 points
- May take any of the following:
  - Sempiternal weave .... 15 points
  - Mindshackle scarabs .... 20 points
  - Tachyon arrow .... 30 points
  - Resurrection orb .... 30 points

HQ

ROYAL COURT

For each Necron Overlord in your army (including Nemesor Zahndrekh, Imotekh the Stormlord, Trazyn the Infinite and Anrakyr the Traveller), the army can also include a Royal Court. This unit does not take up an HQ choice.

Composition:
- 0-5 Necron Lords
- 0-5 Crypteks

Before the battle, each member of the Royal Court has the option of being split off from his unit and assigned to lead a different unit from the following list: Necron Warriors, Necron Immortals, Lychguard or Deathmarks. Only one member of the Royal Court can join each unit in this manner. Otherwise, they remain part of the Royal Court.

NECRON LORD .... **35 points**   **Page 30**

	WS	BS	S	T	W	I	A	Ld	Sv
Necron Lord	4	4	5	5	1	2	2	10	3+

Composition:
- 1 Necron Lord

Wargear:
- Staff of light

Unit Type:
- Infantry (Character)

Special Rules:
- Ever-living
- Reanimation Protocols

Options:
- May exchange staff of light for one of the following:
  - Hyperphase sword .... free
  - Gauntlet of fire .... 5 points
  - Voidblade .... 10 points
  - Warscythe .... 10 points
- Take any of the following:
  - Sempiternal weave .... 15 points
  - Mindshackle scarabs .... 15 points
  - Tesseract labyrinth .... 20 points
  - Resurrection orb .... 30 points
  - Phase shifter .... 45 points

CRYPTEK .... **25 points**   **Page 32**

	WS	BS	S	T	W	I	A	Ld	Sv
Cryptek	4	4	4	4	1	2	1	10	4+

Composition:
- 1 Cryptek

Wargear:
- Staff of light

Unit Type:
- Infantry (Character)

Special Rules:
- Ever-living
- Reanimation Protocols

Options:
- *Upgrade to a Harbinger of Despair, exchanging staff of light for abyssal staff .... 5 points
  - May then take any of the following:
    - Nightmare shroud .... 10 points
    - Veil of darkness .... 30 points
- *Upgrade to a Harbinger of Destruction, exchanging staff of light for eldritch lance .... 10 points
  - May then take any of the following:
    - Gaze of flame .... 10 points
    - Solar pulse .... 20 points
- *Upgrade to a Harbinger of Eternity, exchanging staff of light for aeonstave .... free
  - May then take any of the following:
    - Chronometron .... 15 points
    - Timesplinter cloak .... 30 points
- *Upgrade to a Harbinger of the Storm, exchanging staff of light for voltaic staff .... free
  - May then take any of the following:
    - Lightning field .... 10 points
    - Ether crystal .... 15 points
- *Upgrade to a Harbinger of Transmogrification, exchanging staff of light for tremorstave .... 5 points
  - May then take any of the following:
    - Seismic crucible .... 10 points
    - Harp of dissonance .... 25 points

* Any number of Crypteks that are in a Royal Court can be upgraded to a single, specific type of Harbinger. Whilst you can have any number of Harbingers of a specific type, each of the Harbinger's unique wargear options can only be chosen once in each Royal Court (see page 84).

TROOPS

NECRON WARRIORS .... 65 points

Page 33

	WS	BS	S	T	W	I	A	Ld	Sv
Necron Warrior	4	4	4	4	1	2	1	10	4+

Composition:
- 5 Necron Warriors

Wargear:
- Gauss flayer

Unit Type:
- Infantry

Special Rules:
- Reanimation Protocols

Options:
- May include up to fifteen additional Necron Warriors .... *13 points per model*

Transport:
- May select either a Ghost Ark or Night Scythe as a dedicated transport (see page 91 for points costs).

NECRON IMMORTALS .... 85 points

Page 34

	WS	BS	S	T	W	I	A	Ld	Sv
Necron Immortal	4	4	4	4	1	2	1	10	3+

Composition:
- 5 Immortals

Wargear:
- Gauss blaster

Unit Type:
- Infantry

Special Rules:
- Reanimation Protocols

Options:
- May include up to five additional Necron Immortals .... *17 points per model*
- The entire squad may exchange gauss blasters for tesla carbines .... *free*

Transport:
- May select a Night Scythe as a dedicated transport (see page 91 for points costs).

DEDICATED TRANSPORTS

CATACOMB COMMAND BARGE .... 80 points

Page 52

	BS	Armour F	Armour S	Armour R
Catacomb Command Barge	4	11	11	11

Composition:
- 1 Catacomb Command Barge

Unit Type:
- Vehicle (Fast, Open-topped, Skimmer)

Transport Capacity:
- 1 Independent Character

Wargear:
- Quantum shielding
- Tesla cannon

Special Rules:
- Living Metal
- Sweep Attack
- Symbiotic Repair

Options:
- May exchange tesla cannon for gauss cannon .... *free*

GHOST ARK .... 115 points

Page 53

	BS	Armour F	Armour S	Armour R
Ghost Ark	4	11	11	11

Composition:
- 1 Ghost Ark

Unit Type:
- Vehicle (Open-topped, Skimmer)

Transport Capacity:
- 10 models

Wargear:
- Quantum shielding
- Two gauss flayer arrays

Special Rules:
- Living Metal
- Repair Barge

NIGHT SCYTHE .... 100 points

Page 51

	BS	Armour F	Armour S	Armour R
Night Scythe	4	11	11	11

Composition:
- 1 Night Scythe

Unit Type:
- Vehicle (Fast, Skimmer)

Transport Capacity:
- 15 models

Wargear:
- Twin-linked tesla destructor

Special Rules:
- Aerial Assault
- Deep Strike
- Living Metal
- Supersonic

ELITES

DEATHMARKS .... 95 points   Page 36

	WS	BS	S	T	W	I	A	Ld	Sv
Deathmark	4	4	4	4	1	2	1	10	3+

Composition:
• 5 Necron Deathmarks

Unit Type:
• Infantry

Wargear:
• Synaptic disintegrator

Special Rules:
• Deep Strike
• Ethereal Interception
• Hunters from Hyperspace
• Reanimation Protocols

Options:
• May include up to five additional
  Necron Deathmarks .... *19 points per model*

Transport:
• May select a Night Scythe as a dedicated transport (see
  page 91 for points costs).

LYCHGUARDS .... 200 points   Page 35

	WS	BS	S	T	W	I	A	Ld	Sv
Lychguard	4	4	5	5	1	2	2	10	3+

Composition:
• 5 Lychguards

Unit Type:
• Infantry

Wargear:
• Warscythe

Special Rules:
• Reanimation Protocols

Options:
• May include up to five
  additional Lychguards .... *40 points per model*
• The entire squad may exchange warscythes for hyperphase
  swords and dispersion shields .... *5 points per model*

Transport:
• May select a Night Scythe as a dedicated transport (see
  page 91 for points costs).

TRIARCH PRAETORIANS .... 200 points   Page 38

	WS	BS	S	T	W	I	A	Ld	Sv
Triarch Praetorian	4	4	5	5	1	2	1	10	3+

Composition:
• 5 Triarch Praetorians

Unit Type:
• Jump Infantry

Wargear:
• Rod of covenant

Special Rules:
• Fearless
• Reanimation Protocols

Options:
• May include up to five additional
  Triarch Praetorians .... *40 points per model*
• The entire squad may exchange rod of covenant for
  voidblades and particle casters .... *free*

C'TAN SHARD .... 185 points   Page 40

	WS	BS	S	T	W	I	A	Ld	Sv
C'tan Shard	5	5	7	7	4	4	4	10	4+

Composition:
• 1 C'tan Shard

Unit Type:
• Monstrous Creature
  (Character)

Wargear:
• Necrodermis

Special Rules:
• Fearless
• Eternal Warrior
• Immune to Natural Law

Options:
• Must take two of the following Manifestations of Power
  (only one of each can be taken per army):
    - Entropic Touch .... *10 points*
    - Lord of Fire .... *10 points*
    - Pyreshards .... *15 points*
    - Swarm of Spirit Dust .... *20 points*
    - Moulder of Worlds .... *25 points*
    - Sentient Singularity .... *30 points*
    - Writhing Worldscape .... *35 points*
    - Grand Illusion .... *40 points*
    - Time's Arrow .... *40 points*
    - Transdimensional Thunderbolt .... *45 points*
    - Gaze of Death .... *50 points*

ELITES

FLAYED ONE PACK..65 points   Page 37

	WS	BS	S	T	W	I	A	Ld	Sv
Flayed One	4	1	4	4	1	2	3	10	4+

Composition:
• 5 Flayed Ones

Unit Type:
• Infantry

Special Rules:
• Deep Strike
• Infiltrate
• Reanimation Protocols

Options:
• May include up to
  15 additional Flayed Ones...........................*13 points per model*

TRIARCH STALKER...150 points   Page 39

				┌ Armour ┐			
	WS	BS	S	F	S	R	I	A
Triarch Stalker	4	4	7	11	11	11	2	3

Composition:
• 1 Triarch Stalker

Unit Type:
• Vehicle (Open-topped, Walker)

Wargear:
• Heat ray
• Quantum shielding

Special Rules:
• Living Metal
• Move Through Cover
• Targeting Relay

Options:
• May exchange heat ray for one of the following:
  - Particle shredder...*5 points*
  - Twin-linked heavy gauss cannon............................*15 points*

FAST ATTACK

CANOPTEK WRAITHS .... 35 points   Page 44

	WS	BS	S	T	W	I	A	Ld	Sv
Canoptek Wraith	4	4	6	4	2	2	3	10	3+

Composition:
- 1 Canoptek Wraith

Unit Type:
- Jump Infantry

Wargear:
- Phase shifter

Special Rules:
- Fearless
- Phase Attacks
- Wraithflight

Options:
- May include up to five additional
  Canoptek Wraiths .... *35 points per model*
- Any model may take one of the following:
  - Particle caster .... *5 points per model*
  - Whip coils .... *10 points per model*
  - Transdimensional beamer .... *15 points per model*

CANOPTEK SCARABS .... 45 points   Page 45

	WS	BS	S	T	W	I	A	Ld	Sv
Canoptek Scarabs	2	2	3	3	3	2	4	10	5+

Composition:
- 3 Canoptek Scarab bases

Unit Type:
- Beasts

Special Rules:
- Entropic Strike
- Fearless
- Swarms

Options:
- May include up to seven additional
  Canoptek Scarab bases .... *15 points per base*

TOMB BLADES .... 20 points   Page 42

	WS	BS	S	T	W	I	A	Ld	Sv
Tomb Blade	4	4	4	4(5)	1	2	1	10	4+

Composition:
- 1 Tomb Blade

Unit Type:
- Jetbike

Wargear:
- Twin-linked tesla carbine

Special Rules:
- Reanimation Protocols

Options:
- May include up to four additional
  Tomb Blades .... *20 points per model*
- The entire unit may exchange twin-linked tesla carbines for:
  - Twin-linked gauss blasters .... *free*
  - Particle beamers .... *10 points per model*
- The entire unit may take any of the following:
  - Nebuloscopes .... *5 points per model*
  - Shadowlooms .... *10 points per model*
  - Shield vanes .... *10 points per model*

NECRON DESTROYERS .... 40 points   Page 43

	WS	BS	S	T	W	I	A	Ld	Sv
Necron Destroyer	4	4	4	5	1	2	1	10	3+
Heavy Destroyer	4	4	4	5	1	2	1	10	3+

Composition:
- 1 Destroyer

Unit Type:
- Jump Infantry

Wargear:
- Gauss cannon

Special Rules:
- Preferred Enemy (Everything!)
- Reanimation Protocols

Options:
- May include up to four
  additional Necron Destroyers .... *40 points per model*
- May upgrade up to three Necron Destroyers to
  a Heavy Destroyer, exchanging gauss cannon
  for heavy gauss cannon .... *20 points per model*

HEAVY SUPPORT

DOOMSDAY ARK .... 175 points Page 48

	BS	Armour		
		F	S	R
Doomsday Ark	4	11	11	11

Composition:
- 1 Doomsday Ark

Unit Type:
- Vehicle (Open-topped, Skimmer)

Wargear:
- Doomsday cannon
- Two gauss flayer arrays
- Quantum shielding

Special Rules:
- Living Metal

ANNIHILATION BARGE .... 90 points Page 49

	BS	Armour		
		F	S	R
Annihilation Barge	4	11	11	11

Composition:
- 1 Annihilation Barge

Unit Type:
- Vehicle (Open-topped, Skimmer)

Wargear:
- Quantum shielding
- Twin-linked tesla destructor
- Tesla cannon

Special Rules:
- Living Metal

Options:
- May exchange tesla cannon for gauss cannon .... *free*

NECRON MONOLITH .... 200 points Page 47

	BS	Armour		
		F	S	R
Necron Monolith	4	14	14	14

Composition:
- 1 Monolith

Unit Type:
- Vehicle (Heavy*, Tank, Skimmer)

Wargear:
- Eternity gate
- Four gauss flux arcs
- Particle whip

Special Rules:
- Deep Strike*
- Living Metal

DOOM SCYTHE .... 175 points Page 50

	BS	Armour		
		F	S	R
Doom Scythe	4	11	11	11

Composition:
- 1 Doom Scythe

Unit Type:
- Vehicle (Fast, Skimmer)

Wargear:
- Death ray
- Twin-linked tesla destructor

Special Rules:
- Aerial Assault
- Deep Strike
- Living Metal
- Supersonic

CANOPTEK SPYDER .... 50 points Page 46

	WS	BS	S	T	W	I	A	Ld	Sv
Canoptek Spyder	3	3	6	6	3	2	2	10	3+

Composition:
- 1 Canoptek Spyder

Wargear:
- Scarab hive

Unit Type:
- Monstrous Creature

Special Rules:
- Fearless

Options:
- May include up to two additional Canoptek Spyders .... *50 points per model*
- Any Canoptek Spyder may take a fabricator claw array .... *10 points per model*
- Any Canoptek Spyder may take a gloom prism .... *15 points per model*
- Any Canoptek Spyder may take a twin-linked particle beamer .... *25 points per model*

SUMMARY

MODELS

	WS	BS	S	T	W	I	A	Ld	Sv	Page
Anrakyr the Traveller	4	4	5	5	3	2	3	10	3+	62
Canoptek Scarabs	2	2	3	3	3	2	4	10	5+	45
Canoptek Spyder	3	3	6	6	3	2	2	10	3+	46
Canoptek Wraith	4	4	6	4	2	2	3	10	3+	44
Cryptek	4	4	4	4	1	2	1	10	4+	32
C'tan Shard	5	5	7	7	4	4	4	10	4+	40
Deathmark	4	4	4	4	1	2	1	10	3+	36
Destroyer Lord	4	4	5	6	3	2	3	10	3+	31
Flayed One	4	1	4	4	1	2	3	10	4+	37
Heavy Destroyer	4	4	4	5	1	2	1	10	3+	43
Illuminor Szeras	4	4	4	4	2	2	4	10	3+	56
Imotekh the Stormlord	4	4	5	5	3	2	3	10	2+	54
Lychguard	4	4	5	5	1	2	2	10	3+	35
Necron Destroyer	4	4	4	5	1	2	1	10	3+	43
Necron Immortal	4	4	4	4	1	2	1	10	3+	34
Necron Lord	4	4	5	5	1	2	2	10	3+	30
Necron Overlord	4	4	5	5	3	2	3	10	3+	30
Necron Warrior	4	4	4	4	1	2	1	10	4+	33
Nemesor Zahndrekh	4	4	5	5	3	2	3	10	2+	60
Orikan the Diviner	4	4	4	4	2	2	2	10	4+	57
*Orikan Empowered	5	5	7	7	4	4	4	10	4+	57
Tomb Blade	4	4	4	4(5)	1	2	1	10	4+	42
Trazyn the Infinite	4	4	5	5	3	2	3	10	3+	58
Triarch Praetorian	4	4	5	5	1	2	1	10	3+	38
Vargard Obyron	6	4	5	5	3	2	3	10	2+	60

* These units have additional rules (see the relevant entry).

VEHICLES

	WS	BS	S	Armour Front	Side	Rear	I	A	Page
Annihilation Barge	-	4	-	11	11	11	-	-	49
Catacomb Command Barge	-	4	-	11	11	11	-	-	52
Doom Scythe	-	4	-	11	11	11	-	-	50
Doomsday Ark	-	4	-	11	11	11	-	-	48
Ghost Ark	-	4	-	11	11	11	-	-	53
Necron Monolith	-	4	-	14	14	14	-	-	47
Night Scythe	-	4	-	11	11	11	-	-	51
Triarch Stalker	4	4	7	11	11	11	2	3	39

CRYPTEK WEAPONS

Weapon	Range	Str	AP	Type	Page
Abyssal staff	Template	8	1	Assault 1 Shroud of Despair	84
Eldritch lance	36"	8	2	Assault 1	84
Harp of dissonance	∞ (Infinite)	6	-	Assault 1, Entropic Strike	85
Tremorstave	36"	4	-	Assault 1, Blast, Quake	85
Voltaic staff	12"	5	-	Assault 4, Haywire	85

WEAPONS

Weapon	Range	Str	AP	Type	Page
Death ray	12"	10	1	Heavy 1	50
Doomsday cannon					
Stationary	72"	9	1	Heavy 1, Large Blast	48
Combat speed	24"	7	4	Heavy 1, Blast	48
Eternity gate					
Portal of exile	D6"	X	-	Heavy 1, Special	47
Gauntlet of fire	Template	4	5	Assault 1	81
Gauss blaster	24"	5	4	Rapid Fire, Gauss	8
Gauss cannon	24"	5	3	Assault 2, Gauss	81
Gauss flayer	24"	4	5	Rapid Fire, Gauss	81
Gauss flux arc	24"	4	5	Heavy 3, Gauss*	81
Heat ray					
Focussed	24"	8	1	Heavy 2, Melta	39
Dispersed	Template	5	4	Heavy 1	39
Heavy gauss cannon	36"	9	2	Assault 1, Gauss	81
Particle beamer	24"	6	5	Heavy 1, Blast	81
Particle caster	12"	6	5	Pistol	81
Particle shredder	24"	7	4	Heavy 1, Large Blast	81
Particle whip	24"	8	3	Ordnance 1, Large Blast	81
Rod of covenant	6"	5	2	Assault 1	38
Staff of light	12"	5	3	Assault 3	82
Staff of the Destroyer	2D6"*	6	1	Assault 1, One use only	55
Synaptic disintegrator	24"	X	5	Rapid Fire, Sniper	36
Tachyon arrow	∞ (Infinite)	10	1	Assault 1	82
Tesla cannon	24"	6	-	Assault 2, Tesla	82
Tesla carbine	24"	5	-	Assault 1, Tesla	82
Tesla destructor	24"	7	-	Assault 4, Tesla, Arc	82
Transdimensional beamer	12"	X	-	Heavy 1, Exile Ray	82

* These weapons have additional rules (see the relevant entry).

C'TAN POWERS

Power	Range	Str	AP	Type	Page
Pyreshards	18"	4	-	Assault 8	41
Moulder of Worlds	24"	4	-	Assault 1, Large Blast	41
Transdimensional Thunderbolt	24"	9	2	Assault 1	41